THE PUNCH BOOK OF WOMEN

**Also edited by William Davis,
and available in Coronet Books:**

The Punch Guide to Good Living
The Punch Bedside Book

Copyright © 1973 by Punch Publications Limited
First published by Punch Publications Limited 1973
Coronet edition 1974

Printed and bound in Great Britain for
Coronet Books,
Hodder Paperbacks Ltd,
St. Paul's House, Warwick Lane,
London, EC4P 4AH
by Compton Printing Ltd
Pembroke Road,
Stocklake,
Aylesbury, Bucks
and bound by Hazell Watson & Viney Ltd
Aylesbury, Bucks

ISBN 0 340 18215 6

The Punch Book
of Women

Edited by
William Davis

CORONET BOOKS
Hodder Paperbacks Ltd., London

CONTENTS

INTRODUCTION

PUNCH has been accused of many things in its long life, but the one charge which has stuck with us throughout the 131 years of our existence is that we are defiantly male. Well no, that's putting it too politely. The women's libbers who picketed our office last year were more blunt: they called us male chauvinist pigs. I'm not sure who first thought up that elegant phrase, or even what it means, but I do know that Punch gave ample space to female contributors long before any of today's angry young women were born. In fact, our record is a great deal better than that of many of the magazines who cater almost exclusively for female interests.

This book—successor to the Punch Bedside Book and the Punch Guide to Good Living—should help to prove the point. It's main purpose, though, is much more simple—to entertain and, we sincerely hope, to give you a few laughs. The protesting ladies will no doubt object: at that demo they distributed pamphlets which asked this portentious question: *"Do you believe women are a joke and their problems food for humour?"*

Dear me, no. Not half as much of a joke as we men, anyway. But *everything* is food for humour. God help us if we ever cease to recognise absurdity in human behaviour or laugh at our shortcomings. And whatever gave them the notion that humour isn't a serious business? Swift, Orwell, Shaw and other writers have, surely, demonstrated that, properly used, it is an enormously powerful weapon. More powerful, certainly, than anger.

I have included a number of cartoons published several decades ago to show how things have changed, for better or for worse. And although much of the written work consists of articles by women contributors, I have also dared to include some male observations on the fairer sex. (I refuse to say "weaker" because that would be patently absurd.) If the final outcome suggests an obsession with the domestic and social scene—well, that is what most women's lives are all about. There are as many jokes—elsewhere—about the follies of men.

Sadly, the cartoons are mostly drawn by males. There are at least 30 good cartoonists in Britain, and all but three or four of them are men. I have no idea why this should be so. It certainly isn't because of any bias. When I choose cartoons for Punch I don't ask whether they were drawn by men or women. The only criterion is whether they are likely to make readers laugh.

I've asked a lot of women what they think is the explanation. The answer may surprise you: women, they say, are not very good at humour because they take life more seriously than men. One woman journalist put it like this: "We think —perhaps misguidedly—we ought to set the world right instead of, as a man can, frittering the space away".

I've heard the same sort of comment in other countries, including the United States and Russia. You'll find very few female humorists in the U.S.: the field is totally dominated by men. And when I was guest of Krokodil, the Soviet humour magazine, in Moscow some time ago I found only one woman cartoonist among their team of more than forty contributors. This in a country where more than half the university graduates and the majority of doctors are women.

Ah, you may counter, but what about comediennes like Lucille Ball? Surely they are funny? Yes, as *performers*. They have the looks, the timing, and the delivery which together make for success. But the most important ingredient is the script—and that is invariably written by men. In Britain, the pace has been set by the Goons, Michael Bentine, Frank Muir and Denis Norden, Galton and Simpson, Johnny Speight, the cast of Beyond the Fringe, and the regulars on Monty Python's Flying Circus. All men. And yet comedy writing, like cartooning, is no closed shop. The usual women's lib arguments don't apply. Good comedy writers are in such demand that no-one would turn down a really funny script simply because it came from a woman.

To me, the really odd thing about all this is that most of the women I know personally have a highly developed sense of the ridiculous. They are closer to the real world and, because of this, less pretentious and hypocritical. There is nothing more devastating than a woman who can see through male posturing—and expose it with a single, cutting remark. The following pages also demonstrate, I think, that women can write every bit as well as men—if not better.

Why, then, does so little of it come out in public? Why do even the most obvious platforms—women's magazines and the women's pages of daily newspapers—have so little time for humour? Perhaps that woman journalist is right about the basic seriousness of her sex. Or perhaps it's true that, as one woman reader suggested in a long (and serious) letter, "women are hilariously funny when they feel comfortably free to be so knowing that no man is within earshot".

I leave you to judge. All I can tell you is that, throughout the past year, male readers have complained that their wives appropriated the Punch Guide to Good Living as soon as it reached them, and that they haven't seen it since. Say what you like, women make splendidly appreciative readers. Perhaps the men should retaliate with this year's offering—if they dare.

WILLIAM DAVIS

Women in a Man's World

Marghanita Laski

1. Video Something-or-Other

WHAT it means to be a woman and not a man is something I wish I knew. I know what the complementary physical differences are, and that of some of them men have been known to cry *vive!* It's perfectly possible that from these physical differences depend some mental, social, temperamental differences as innate as they, but what they are I have never been able to determine. No sooner do I think of an apparent non-physical difference between men and women than qualifications leap up and hit me in the face—"Yes, but in Sparta, on the Zambesi, in Elizabethan England, among the working classes . . ."

In the end the only differences between men and women that I can pinpoint—no, not pinpoint, rather point a shaking finger at a great quivering blot—are those that more or less prevail among people of more or less my own age and class living in roughly the same neighbourhood and engaged in something like the same sorts of activities, and even in such a tiny group as this no statement can be dogmatically made without provisos. And there isn't one difference I can adduce that isn't at least as likely to be the result of social conditioning as of innate sexual differentiation.

So what, as it seems to me, it all eventually comes down to is differing social conventions for men and for women, and these themselves differing not only as between the sexes as a whole, but as between different classes, ages, regions, avocations, periods of time, and each of these admitting enough exceptions to disprove the possibility of any rule. Certainly there is a range of conventions I accept as proper to my role of married, maternal, middle-aged, middle-class, mid-twentieth-century English writer, and the more unquestioningly I accept them, the more trivial they prove to be.

Many of the least questioned are to do with children, which perhaps helps to sustain the point about conditioning being more significant than any innate propensities. I wouldn't dream of buying a pink rattle for a boy or a blue one for a girl, though I'm told the French do it the other way round: I wouldn't, unless specifically requested, buy a toy train for a girl or a doll for a boy. In the kinds of games where little boys bow and little girls curtsey, I wouldn't try to reverse or muddle the roles. And I might quite well say things like "Boys don't hit girls" without pausing to consider that, as an accepted rule of actual conduct, the reverse is at least as true if not truer.

Differences of dress there certainly are, and the more formal the occasion, the greater the differences. At play or at progressive schools, the children of my class, etc., tend to be dressed alike as, at week-ends or in the country, are their parents. Hierarchical schools dress the sexes differently. Parties, at least for the very young and middle-aged, dress the sexes differently. So does white-collar work, and so, appropriately, do those most formal and sex-differentiated occasions of all, white weddings.

But except for very formal occasions and/or very specific moments in time, it would be hard to be dogmatic as to what differences in get-up are. Trousers in Europe are surely men's wear adopted by women, but beyond that one hardly dare go. Men who don't use cosmetics-for-men might claim they're the non-cosmetic-using sex, but this is only because they don't count what they do use (hair lotion, for instance) as cosmetics. Besides, as advertisers dolefully wail, lots of women don't seem to be the cosmetic-using sex either.

Most men hold doors open for women and walk into restaurants either before or after women, I'm never sure which. Men often light cigarettes for women, seldom, now, give up seats to them in buses or trains. Men who are trying to make women usually pay for them when they take them out. Some men say they like working with women and some say they don't. In either sense, this isn't usually an appropriate statement from women.

When it comes to married life, most well-working couples settle for a functional division of tasks, usually following traditional patterns. In my class, etc., men are usually the primary earners, but most women earn too. The pattern of living is still, however, far more often determined, geographically and socially, by the man's job, though this is, fairly enough, often reversed when the woman's job is substantially more lucrative or important. Many more men inherit jobs (e.g. to do with land or commerce) than women do; I suspect they inherit more money too. In the home, women usually do the minute-by-minute, hour-by-hour jobs and purchases, men the larger ones, but with many exceptions. Men usually carve but don't buy the roast, usually both buy and serve drinks; in fact, the whole mystique of alcoholic drink is almost entirely a male ploy. Nowadays men often cook (though seldom where there are seven children and a limited income) and I find I don't usually care for the ones that do, or greatly for their cooking which tends to be over-finicky and incapable of leaving good food to taste for itself.

As drink to men, so linen-cupboards to women. Not all women are devoted to their linen, but I've never met a man who was. The nearest they get is demanding best linen sheets.

Of little fiddly unstable differences like these there are plenty, but of great big role-determining instead of role-determined ones, what? Are women more cultured and religious? No, but women traditionally "do" the culture and the religion. Are women less good at maths? Probably not, look at Mary Somerville, but most only recently taught it. Are women more loving, tender, sensitive? I don't think so, but we're trained to behave as if we were. Are women, as the women's papers and many do-gooders say, incapable of sex without total emotional commitment? I've never believed this myself, convinced that the ways people act about love in sex are as socially conditioned as most other things about them. Are women the weaker sex? Well, we die less often in infancy and seem to live longer, though the latter may be due to social conditions; I should suppose that most of us weren't as capable as most men of very heavy work.

I once read that except in bed the Chinese consider differences between males and females irrelevant. This seems to me sensible, and probably in accordance with what look as if they may be the facts. Men and women have, inescapably, complementary physical differences. By custom and conditioning they are socially, temperamentally and mentally differentiated. But actually, I would guess, they differ far more as individuals than they do as men and women.

2. The Female Virtues

WHAT the female virtues traditionally are we all know: Chastity, first and foremost, for all respectable girls, transformed into unswerving fidelity after marriage; and for mistresses and tarts, generosity. Obedience is, I think, the next most important, applying to all women alike, because all women are ideally seen as handmaids or servants; obedience does not exclude, of course, a certain tantalising rebellion on appropriate occasions, so long as there's no question but it will be firmly and pleasurably mastered. I think there could be sense as well as tidiness in including poverty, the third of the triad of monkish virtues, since it has been proper for women to be financially dependent on men. If, by good fortune, they inherited property, they were married for it and handed it over willy-nilly; if, on the mistress side of the blanket, they amassed it, it was only at the expense of and by giving pleasure to men; and once married, decent economy was the duty.

But if poverty, chastity and obedience sufficed for monks, much more in Western European society was asked of women. There was the ministering angel aspect, which applied to all classes and degrees of respectability. There was the helpmeet aspect, and with it the whole day-to-day burden of bearing the responsibilities of family life towards whatever generations might be dependent. Then, for anyone with any pretensions of gentility, there was the living up to whatever was the contemporary interpretation of that confused concept, ladylikeness. In recent history this has covered such things as daintiness, fastidiousness, nice speaking, formal practices as regards the conventions, some pretension to culture (which was certainly not the same thing as education), and maintaining the moral, religious and social standards of the family.

Before we ask which, if any, of these female virtues are relevant today, it is proper to ask whether any specifically female virtues are proper. Should there be any differences at all between the virtues practised by men and the virtues practised by women?

I think there probably should be, not, perhaps, in gross but in particular. Most virtues are, of course, proper to all human beings, courage, say, and honesty and kindness, but even so there may well be differences in the proper method of their practice by one sex and by the other. What is demanded, I suppose, is that we each practise as best we can the virtues appropriate to our function; or, to use a well-tried axiom, that we do our duty in the station of life to which it may please God (or accident or effort) to call us, always bearing in mind that some stations in life are intolerable and that in them the right duty may be rebellion. (Which is, apparently, what many adolescents feel today about the station in life of being an adolescent.)

Inescapably, women, by virtue of being women and the child-bearing sex, are mostly called to different stations in life, from men and to some extent probably always will be. Moreover, in today's social set-up, the station of a wife is inescapably different in many respects from the station of a husband. For most women, though nowadays not necessarily for all, the virtues called for by duty are complementary to, not the same as, the duties of men.

Of these virtues perhaps the most interesting, and the one most under fire today, is that of chastity. On the face of it the need for chastity must be greater in women than in men, however much a sense of justice screams disavowal. Certainly both sexes, by unchastity, can taint each other and future generations with disease. Both sexes, by arousing the irrational and often uncontrollable jealousy of infidelity, can bring destruction on themselves and on the family. Both sexes, through unchastity, contribute to the conception of children who may be born illegitimate. But it is the women who must actually bear the illegitimate child and usually take responsibility for it, and to bring illegitimate, or, indeed, unwanted, children into the world is coming to seem to me almost the worst of social sins.

More and more we are coming to learn that the illegitimate or unwanted child is far more likely than others to become a social liability, a misery to itself and to society and to the future generations it is liable to breed. And so I should say that above the obligations of chastity for both sexes, in so far as both sexes have an obligation to avoid disease and jealous disruption of relations, a modern interpretation of chastity in women must be the absolute avoidance of illegitimate childbearing. I would add that I believe that anyone who tries to prevent this, by preventing birth control knowledge or abortion, is doing wrong.

The positive side of the negative virtue of chastity comprises, in one or another modified form, almost all the traditional female virtues. The positive side is, of course, the maintenance of the family, the hour-to-hour, day-to-day job that few men can do because they're not there to do it. It is women who must basically ensure the security of the home, establish not only its physical provisions like food and cleanliness and comfort but also its spiritual atmosphere. Nor must it be forgotten that women's duty is not only to their children but to their husbands.

As things are and for a long time seem likely to be, the old concepts remain valid to a surprising extent. If differences between sexual virtues have diminished before the establishment of the family, once this has happened most of the older virtues hold sway. Women have their own property now, probably their own earned property, but as it is they who do over ninety per cent of the nation's day-to-day buying, the duty of poverty—of economy, at least as opposed to splash—must still fall on them. We interpret culture more widely than past generations did, and certainly today it must include education, but still culture, in the best broadest sense of the term, must largely be transmitted by the women because they are there in the home to do it. And for the same reason, the ministering-angel aspect, essential in any family, must still largely fall on them, ministering not only to children but to husband and probably a lot of other people as well. Among the many things a good home should be is a refuge, and this aspect must be of prime importance to the husband who usually, for many more years than the wife, must leave it to work, come back to it tired to be refreshed.

In *The Grapes of Wrath* John Steinbeck has the wives of the Oklahoma farmers, after each terrible season of drought, anxiously watching the men to see if they break. They, the women, can, they know, endure. So long as the men don't break, life and the family can go on.

I said in my first article that I know of no innate differences between men and women but the physical ones. Knowing and believing are, however, two different things, and I believe in my bones that women are the stronger sex in this sense of having greater endurance, being less likely to break. So in the last resort I believe that the most characteristic, the most vital of the female virtues is to take care of men.

You men have run things long enough, Pete, but us sisters don't feel inferior anymore! We want fulfilment!

EQUALITY NOW

HOT DOGS

Call Me Madam at Your Peril!

William Davis

San Francisco

ELMO R. Zumwalt Junior has been making trouble. Elmo is an Admiral: indeed he is America's Chief of Naval Operations. And he has just lifted the ban against women serving aboard warships at sea.

The news has produced fierce protests—from women. Several hundred Navy wives have signed a petition urging the Admiral to change his mind. "I wouldn't want my daughter going out in hand-to-hand combat," one told the *New York Times.* Another thought that having women aboard would be unfair to the men: "They're not going to be able to relax."

The episode again shows that, whatever Women's Lib may say, men are not the only enemy. Indeed, they may not even be the principal opponents.

Many American women resent the activities of ardent feminists, and are becoming increasingly vocal. They go along with the more serious causes (equal pay, child-care centres, equal rights in law) but dislike the uncompromising aggressiveness of the self-appointed freedom fighters. "I was with them at first," one young female radio producer told me here. "But I got turned off by their rhetoric. A lot of them are more interested in words than in action. And some of their causes are just plain silly."

One mistake made by Women's Lib, it seems, has been to show open contempt for "sisters" who actually like to stay at home. The role of the modern housewife, it is pointed out, is far from being as one-dimensional and stultifying as Women's Lib makes it out to be. Many busy housewives find their lives a good deal more varied than their husbands' working day. And they *enjoy* cooking, needlework and other pursuits derided by the feminists.

Women's Lib may also have erred in ignoring the fact that men, too, often have boring and unfulfilling jobs. Anthropologist Sheila K. Johnson ("my own field has never discriminated against women") notes that "feminists, when they lobby for greater access to male occupations, always seem to cast their argument in terms of highly visible, satisfying careers such as those of doctors, lawyers, university professors or journalists. They never stop to consider that for every one such job there are at least ten which consist of working on an assembly line, driving a truck or bus, or clerking in a store."

15

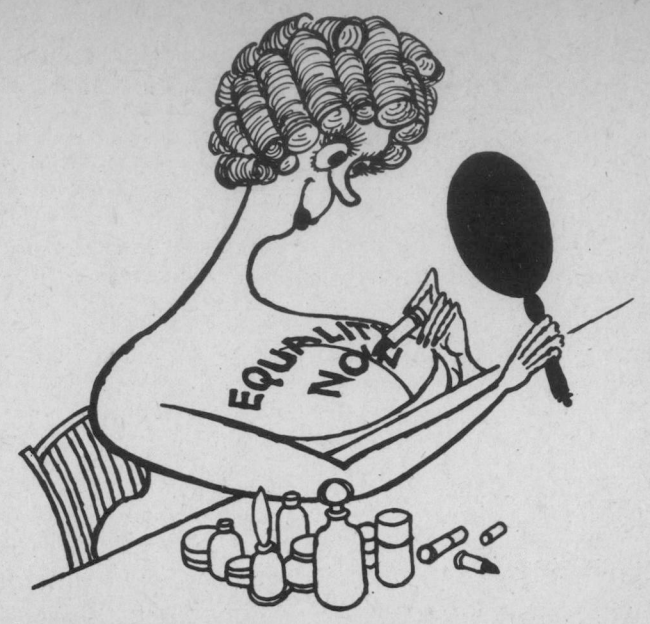

Good propagandists don't score points for the other side, but by refusing to acknowledge such obvious points—and meeting them with arguments—Women's Lib has tended to look self-centred and unfair. Critics have also been quick to point out that feminists, too, discriminate when it suits them. Some of New York's feminist theatre groups will not admit men nor perform for them. And *Ms.*, the new Women's Lib magazine, does not have a single man on its editorial staff. "How," wrote one irate reader in the August issue, "can a group of women, who have been working for equality of the sexes, have a staff of publisher, editors and associates which includes not even one male? . . . Such blatant disregard for the rights of members of the other sex is apt to have the frequently hurled epithet of 'male chauvinist pigs' rebound as 'female chauvinist sows'."

The editors offer what may strike you as a feeble excuse. Is it upsetting or illegal, they ask, that almost all the employees of *Ebony* or *Black Scholar* are black? There is, they add, a legal term for these and other jobs that, for cultural or physical reasons, should be filled by one sex: B.F.O.Q. or Bona Fide Occupational Qualification, was invented by the Equal Employment Opportunities Commission to describe just such needs.

Oh yes?

None of these things would matter if militant women were not quite so dogmatic or so journalistic in their choice of language. Women's Lib is self-righteous, intolerant, and angry. Most of its leaders are journalists who seem more interested in finding an "angle" that will sell to editors and publishers than in getting worthwhile results. The angles are becoming increasingly extravagant. What can one say about headlines like "The Liberated Orgasm" or "Sexist Religion hit by Women Theologians"? The current issue of *The Washingtonian* looks at "Our Biggest Male Chauvinist Pigs," and lists "Fifteen Prime Porkers Plus a Blue Ribbon Hog." The hog is, of course, Richard Nixon—who, the author claims, "clings nostalgically to a patristic view of a strong family unit with the father as the breadwinner and dominant figure." Well, most American women probably share his view.

Quoting the dictionary, *The Washingtonian* defines a chauvinist as "A person unreasonably devoted to his own race, sex, etc. and contemptuous of other races, the opposite sex, etc." The trouble with Women's Lib is that, in its eagerness to keep the bandwagon rolling, it is in danger of being itself branded as chauvinist.

One of the sillier causes is the argument about "sexist language." When women get worked up about hurricanes having feminine names, and suggest words like "mistress-piece" for the writings of a Virginia Woolf, Women's Lib tends to take a step backwards. There is no reason why we should not have chairwomen, and I dare say we could bring ourselves to name hurricanes "George" instead of "Agnes." But these are trivial issues, detracting from the very real arguments which gave birth to Women's Lib.

It may be that, as blacks have always argued, gimmicks and extremist attitudes produce a significant change at the centre. There is certainly more awareness of women's rights than there was five years ago. A George McGovern would not have bothered to make it a major election issue during the sixties. And a Richard Nixon would certainly not have gone out of

his way to proclaim August 26th "Women's Rights Day". Not least, the business world would not be half as keen to have the "obligatory woman," as well as the obligatory black, among its executive staff. Tokenism is here to stay—thanks to Black Power and Women's Lib.

But tokenism is not enough. Women's Lib rightly insists on equality. The trouble is that the world is not divided by sex: the notion that all men are treated as equal simply does not stand up. Women who fail to secure desirable jobs tend to argue that discrimination is to blame, even when it clearly isn't. Unless they are black, men have no such excuse. And many are irritated by the angry complaints of female militants who, more often than not, come from privileged homes.

The irritation is shared by women who cannot be dismissed as "morons". The months ahead will see the publication of several books which take a caustic second look at Women's Lib: one, by Midge Decter, is billed as a "Counter-Revolution."

Privately, some of the militants concede that their biggest enemies are not men, but "sisters" who refuse to see the light. They are notoriously rough on other women, especially if they happen to be in junior positions, or if they look like becoming a serious rival. Career women tend to be more suspicious, and far less easily swayed, than their male colleagues.

Wives are, if anything, worse. And not just in the Navy. Many wives of top executives—the people who make key appointments—do their best to keep attractive and intelligent women away from their husbands, because they know how easily men are led astray. It would be interesting to know how

SEXIST!

many high level jobs have been approved by men and vetoed by jealous wives back home. There certainly is no doubt that fields like fashion and hair-dressing are dominated by men because female customers want it that way. They prefer to buy clothes designed by men, just as they prefer to deal with male bankers and lawyers and watch male newscasters on TV. The militants know this and find it frustrating. They do not concede it because, they say, it would weaken their case.

Is Women's Lib over the hill? In New York, on the newly proclaimed Women's Rights day, there was an impressive parade led by three women motorcyclists and a fife-and-drum team. But the number of marchers was less than half that of two years before. And there are signs that both the press and television have become bored with the movement. It's going to be harder, in future, to attract attention. In California, right now, Women's Lib is getting virtually no publicity. More fuss is being made of ridiculous issues like "Systematic Discrimination" against waterbeds and their owners by land-lords. An organisation calling itself Patriotic American Citizens for Waterbed Rights has started a legal campaign, and is getting considerable press support. The feminists still argue, but people are less inclined to listen. Women's Lib has ceased to be a novelty.

Somehow I feel like
I've just personally set
women's lib back
ten thousand years!

Perhaps it's just as well. By concentrating on the trivial, the militants have obscured the more important causes and invited ridicule. By treating all men as enemies, they have alienated potential supporters. A less flamboyant approach could well turn out to be more productive.

George McGovern has accused Richard Nixon of treating the women's movement "as a joke". Nixon has countered by issuing an elaborate fact sheet which shows that three times as many women now work in top Government jobs as four years ago. There is not, as yet, any woman politician who stands a serious chance of becoming President, or even Vice-President, in 1976. But women are more of a political force in America than ever before. An unprecedented number are running for Congress, and for judgeships, local offices and seats in the State Legislature. By no means all of them, however, are ardent feminists. And an even greater number of women intend to campaign vigorously for the "Blue Ribbon Hog," Richard Nixon. Three dozen wives of Cabinet members and White House officials will soon begin a six-week trip around America to tell their sisters how marvellous—and sadly misunderstood—the President is. "He's just like an uncle," says one of them reassuringly. And that, I suspect, is just what most American women want.

Mrs. Beryl Gooch, of Buddlestone Road, has just completed a replica of the Crown Jewels made from cardboard, wire, old cistern ball-cocks, fly swats and old pearls and beads. It took her eight weeks.   (Kent Messenger)

Most of the women in the class were very conscientious, said Mr. Benning. Two years ago, one of them had made a double bed during the autumn term. After Christmas, the same lady made a cot.   (Henley Standard)

We all need someone, or something, to talk to. I have a friend who talks to her flowers, and another who talks to her sewing. Once, I told her I simply could not ease a sleeve into an armhole. "Talk to it," she advised me seriously. "Coax it and it will go in beautifully." I was inclined to laugh, but—it worked!   (Woman's Own)

The women members of Crosland Moor Darby and Joan Club for over-sixties want more male members of the club. One reason for the shortage, says club leader Mrs. Beatrice Ingham, is "a lot of men are afraid of being trapped by a woman. We have always been short of men. We get a few, and then they die off and we are short again."
                              (Huddersfield Examiner)

In Praise of Girls

by Michael ffolkes

The awfully nice thing about girls is
that even if they are sometimes . . .

. . . slaves to fashion . .

less than Fanny Craddock . . .

. . . idiotic at games . . .

. . . lacking a sense of humour . . .

. . . unfortunate in their choice of parents . . .

. . . unpredictable in their tastes . . .

... over-energetic ...

... one of

... indifferent to machinery ...

... expensive to run ...

... careless about time ...

... ge family ...

... they are **all** sisters under the skin!

SALLY VINCENT
Wants to Know
How Glamour
Ended up in
Carnaby Street

WHEN we were young and uncorrupted, a glamorous man was always common property. The nearest we got to exclusive rights on the thief of our hearts was possession of the Picture-goer cut-out of his crooked grin, sellotaped to the undersides of our desk lids. In our healthy little ways, we were all in thrall to some crown prince of the silver screen or other, and yet we lived in uneasy apprehension of disillusion. How well I remember the crippling stab in the solar plexus that accompanied the taunt, "Kirk Douglas is only five foot four"; and later, when our tastes for toni perms and Mario Lanza matured to more complex susceptibilities, the bitter blow of Peter Ustinov's marriage, e. e. cummings' death and the brave admittance of the fact that even if Gerard Manley Hopkins had been born in the appropriate century he wouldn't have been interested.

They were small anguish, though, in the sense that the magic spells were cast only in our fantasy lives, set far apart from the throes of true ambition. Besides, we were all in it together. We worshipped in girlish groups, giving comprehensive protection to each others' chimerical indulgences, while as individuals we were content to be charmed, like the Snark, by nothing more lavish than smiles and soap. There was a time for being rescued, weak around the legs, by Don Winslow of the Coastguard, and a time for real life sexual adventures. And the two did not impinge on each other. We had our standards. Anything in trousers that was not exactly oozing misogyny and halitosis was regarded as perfectly acceptable. Furthermore, it didn't matter what the trousers were like.

There was no such thing as glamour in real life. Nothing false or fictitious came between us and the pursuit of gratification. A man was a person who might or might not marry us, and sucks to the cut of his jib. A haircut was a haircut, a suit of clothes, a pair of shoes a pair of shoes. Either we liked each other or we didn't. We might as well have crawled round in the dark seeking a mate and trusting solely in our vibes, which as any unglamorous sensualist will agree, is the best way to do it. But those, my dears, those were the days.

These days, alas, most of us live next door to pop stars, albeit manque, and we cannot flee the sting of the humiliating comparison between our own meek attractions and the wondrous trappings of the emergent male. Now everywhere you look, there's a man fairly dripping with glamour. The dolly-boy is with us. He crept up on us with stealthy after-shaves and under-arm deodorants and we thought that was reasonable. He allowed us to wear his nicest shirts. But he stayed to flaunt himself with jewels, with permanent waves and false eyelashes, with floral garments and cachou scented pudenda, coyly outlined within the flimsy fabric of his hand-sewn fly. And he started wearing *our* clothes.

God knows we tried to be liberal about it all. Only doddering old Tory peers with homosexual terrors denounced the trend as effeminate. Nonsense, we said, as we set aside our Betty Friedan, femininity is illusory anyway, so how can you have an illusion of an illusion? So we admire his curls and went out to buy him a pretty necklace. Beauty, we insisted, was only skin deep. And it wasn't for some time that we noticed that he preferred to leave his wallet at home rather than have it clutter up his outline. Beauty, you see, is not skin deep. Surround yourself with enough of it and it seeps right through to the bone. The dolly boy has made himself attractive all right—but to whom? His trappings are so similar to the dolly-girl's that somehow they manage to cancel each other out, desexing one another. One has only to observe the young at their leisure; the rubbing of their peripheries is as dry and as abrasive as a cricket's back legs. Who the hell is the sexual object anyway?

Once upon a time, when the Greeks were naughty pagans, it was necessary for young lads to primp themselves and learn

"What's the idea, dressing like a man?"

winsome ways in order to make themselves attractive to older men, who might otherwise have felt compelled to slaughter the lot of them for failing to pull their weight in the community. So they became cute little tarts and nobody was any the worse off for it. But what, I ask myself, do we need all these cute little tarts for now? And I wouldn't be surprised if sometimes, as they tremulously be-gear themselves for a night out round the dartboard, they ask themselves the same question. There is something so wistful about the dolly boy, so fragile within his Mr. Fish; it is almost as though he was waiting for some kind lady, a well preserved, well heeled, expense accounted for dream mother to sweep him off his boots and give him the keys to her motor car. A Mrs. Stone to touch his perfect body with her mind. If that won't do, who else is left? Only, I venture to suggest, a beautiful reflection in a lonely shaving mirror. Meanwhile, the only people who can afford to smile are the moguls of Carnaby Street, protesting all the way to the bank about the naturalness of the peacock generation.

Clearly, they have never seen a peacock. He, poor bird, was doomed by nature and a lot of fat mandarins to bear the burden of colossal glamour. The people come from far and wide to gasp at his glory in Holland Park, where he is currently engaged in his mating season. It is a tragic sight. There is his wondrous fan, blue and silver irridescence, quivering, swaying, a miracle of exotica in the grey light of W.8. And his neck, gleaming, throbbing, the most intense of all the blues of fairyland. And his crown, atop his delicate head, so exquisite a jewel. And there, there's the peahen, bending her dowdy old head to the dust in bored contemplation of a few old crusts, casting sideways glances of the most total and condemning contempt. She has seen it all before and she knows the true worth of all this parading. Nothing ever happens. Not when I'm watching, anyway. And when, at the height of his ardour he stoops his gleaming fan to the earth, pulsating with the lust of the ages, you can see all his heart-breaking superstructure. The whole thing is put together with match sticks and sellotape, as artless as the tatty behind of an Ivor Novello stage set. Poor peacock, it gets in his way.

". . . Oh, come on Paula . . . I'm sure a lot of women have been mistaken for Danny la Rue . . .!"

Clothes conscious

Shall we Join the Ladies?

MAURICE EDELMAN looks at some vital statistics in the Common Market

WE all know our Metric Man. He's as average as *l'homme moyen sensuel*. He drives up to Heathrow in a Renault, and travels Air France with an Olivetti in one hand and a bottle of Bell's in the other. His first stop is Paris where he will stay in his company's suite at the Georges Cinq; and from there he'll go on to Milan that he knows as well as he does his native Balsall Heath. And although he never learnt French, Italian or German, he speaks all three with gusto. He is forty-four years old, one metre eighty centimetres tall, and has three children, two boys still at school, the girl learning French with a family at Bordeaux.

But what about Metric Man's counter-part, the Common Market woman? Who is she? What does she look like? Well for one thing, she isn't the international model in shorts who twinkles her thighs across the glossies. The Common Market woman is a housewife. I used to think of her, I must admit, as someone like the stout vivandière in Maclise's great fresco, "Waterloo" in Westminster Hall, with her robe slipping off her creamy shoulders as she succours the infantry, French, English, Scots, Russians, Belgians and Italians alike—a woman with the face of a Renaissance Saint or the Bride of the Abydos, untainted by mercenariness and full of compassion.

Somehow or other, I now think that the new European Woman is more of a thruster than Maclise's camp-follower, and I've been hardened in my view by the authoritative survey of the *Reader's Digest* on Europe*. What emerges is a woman who since the Treaty of Rome first came into her life has become steadily more mechanised and homogenised. Instead of stacking stooks or topping up the marmite or thumping the pasta like her land-girl mother, the new woman of the Six has joined her own liberation movement where she commands the prepackaged benefits of the post-industrial society for cash. The cash-economy has indeed caught up at last with Europen woman and taken her out of the kitchen.

To begin with, she goes out to work. None of that Kinder and Kuche stuff. In West Germany, according to the *Reader's Digest,* 27 per cent of housewives go out to work: in Britain three of every five women between the ages of forty-five and fifty-four. On average, 20 per cent of European households have two wage earners.

Well, the women might say, we always drudged away unpaid at home or on the farm . . . That's just the point.

*A Survey of Europe Today, published by Reader's Digest Association.

Because women now work for cash, they can pay the ransom price of the mechanical gadgets that liberate them from the kitchen or the milking-shed.

"Gadget"—a masculine word that's become one of the most popular words with women in "franglais," the hybrid language of Euro-America. The Common Market woman has gone electronic a decade behind the USA, but the washing-machine, the vacuum cleaner and the washing-up machine have created an electronic sisterhood.

Take Italy. You can forget the tarantellas and fandangos in the piazzas and the arias floating from the coloratura sopranos on the balconies. The typical rhythm of Naples is the whirr of the washing-machine and the hum of the driers. Nearly half of Italy's families has washing-machines compared with only 8 per cent seven years ago.

Mind you, even gadgetry has its priorities. Half the homes of Italy have bathrooms or showers; but nearly three-quarters will soon have TV sets. The French are catching up in the baths department; seven years ago, only one in three had a bath in the home; today one in two.

The real test of cleanliness, though, isn't plumbing but soap. Britain—as you might expect—is far and away the front runner using 1.1 kilo of soap a year per head compared with 0.8 kilo in Germany and Benelux and—surprise—0.8 kilo in sweet-smelling France and hygienic Switzerland. I must admit that I find it a little disillusioning that the new Marianne—the pert-faced mini-skirted image of the modern French cartoonists—should be so short on soap. To think that beneath those dreamily named scents—*Je Reviens, Mon Secret, Aveu, Câline, Shalimar*—oh, never mind! We'll just have to keep an eye on the Consumer charts.

In the meantime, you'll be interested to know that in Italy, habits are changing fast. According to the invaluable

"We've overtaken the Joneses; we're now in full cry after the Crosby-Joneses."

Digest researchers who must have got a black eye or two during their enquiries, 12 per cent of Italian women used deodorants in 1963, compared with 44 per cent today. "Throughout Europe," they add, "mothers appear to be less odour-conscious than their daughters." Humph!

Still, it does illustrate that European woman is changing fast. Today, she is the product of the techniques of the Second Industrial Revolution, modelling herself not on the film-star pacemakers of the past but on the advertisers' artifacts in the European glossies like *Elle*. In town, the Common Market Woman wants to live in a modern flat with a fully equipped electronic kitchen. She wants a flat by the sea with an urbanised hinterland. She needs two cars, two fur coats and three holidays a year. She loves the Consumer Society; her basic reaction to it is, "More!"

"Yes" you may say, "but what does this woman look like?" I must tell you straight away what she doesn't look like. She doesn't look like Miss Bardot who is as remote from her as Madame Curie. She doesn't look like Miss Loren; the American hue is too emphatic. Nor is she to be seen among the models or the tourists in Europe's night spots. Not that she's encumbered by domestic responsibilities. She has 0.86 children. (Remember that more than two-thirds of Belgian households have no children at all.) She is 36 and free to travel. She is self-confident in the presence of her self-confident husband. She speaks loudly and clearly, and her hairdresser is now as important to her as her doctor. She is ill-educated but she rises above her limitations by means of her assertive chatter. She is well content with her husband, and quarrels with him once a month and is unfaithful to him every two years. Her views, if anything, are rather conservative, and significantly the European woman of the Occupied Six has tamed the Nazi jackboots and now wears them with chic.

Oh yes—I was forgetting—her face! Well, it's a bit like Jeanne Moreau's—sullen, pre-occupied, ardent, nostalgic for adventure, the face of a woman who knows very well which side her brioche is buttered. And likes it that way.

"I'm sorry, girls, but I'm in love with another harem."

"It's nice of you to meet me every night Gladys, Eut ..."

33

The Career Wife

HOW TO SUCCEED

Mahood reports

"Your Mummy is something big in the City."

MARION
GRIMSHAW

MANAGING
DIRECTOR

"Hello Mr. Grimshaw, I'm afraid Mrs. Grimshaw hasn't a free date for a visit to your marriage counsellor until mid-November."

"My boss, Mrs. Rankin, will be there, so put on loads of that sexy after-shave of yours."

"I ran your personal data through the computer today and as my Mr. Right you failed miserably on all counts."

"We can't go on meeting like this over a business lunch—couldn't you find time for an occasional evening at home with me and the children?"

"My husband doesn't understand me."

"I do believe in equal pay, Ronald, and I would like to give you a raise, but I don't want to be accused of nepotism."

"Working late again! For God's sake, Myra, what is this, a trial separation?"

"I think I saw an eyelid flicker."

AT THE COSTUMIER'S

CHES GUDENIAN

I KNOW it's the second time you've brought it back, madam, but I'm afraid I can't answer for the zip breaking out. You say you *haven't* put on weight? Well, it probably *was* too tight on the waist; if you breathe in too hard at the fitting, that's what happens, of course. You're not the only one, you know —you'd be surprised how many clients pretend to be Bartoks when they've got a tape measure round their middles. I'll put a new one in, by all means, but it's bound to break out again. No, we can't do *that*—there's nothing to let out, you see . . . well, you only gave me the bare yard and a half, didn't you? I'll do what I can, but it will be a few weeks. I know it's only a small thing, but I've a ball gown to finish for Mrs. Freeman, a theatre coat for Miss Grey and three cocktail dresses for Mrs. Lisle . . .

Oh, this is your material for the afternoon dress, is it? I see . . . And this is the pattern . . . well, it's more of a house frock, really isn't it? Yes, a pretty colour—it was all the rage last season—but I wonder if the material isn't going to seat a bit, especially with the style of skirt you've chosen. Still, it's what you want, and that's the most important thing. Let's just pin it on and see, now . . . and, madam, try to stand the way you always do, just slump a little. . .

All that Glisters May Not Be Gold, But Most of It Is

Indoctrinated from our earliest years, we're bound to grow up prejudiced against rich women. Unfair! cries ALAN COREN, what we need is a few new legends . . .

. . . and lo! the slipper was a perfect fit!

"At last!" cried the handsome Prince. "I have journeyed all the length and breadth of this land, searching for the maiden with the crystal coach and the six white chargers and the liveried footmen, and now I know my search has not been in vain. To think, when I saw no sign of coach or steeds or servants, I almost passed your dwelling by!"

And he laughed, gaily, and pressed Cinderella to his brave bosom, and he held her out at arm's length again, marvelling at her beauty.

And Cinderella laughed aloud for joy.

"Oh, my Prince! That coach was but a pumpkin, the horses mice, the footmen only frogs!"

"Ha, ha, ha!" said the Prince.

"I do not jest," cried Cinderella, for she was as honest as she was beautiful; and she told him of her fairy godmother.

And the Prince's face grew thoughtful, and he stood apart awhile.

"Don't take this the wrong way, kid," he said at last, "but I have my position to consider. Word gets out my fiancee ain't good for more than half a dozen mice and a Hertz coach, what does that make me? Not to mention where the royal purse has seen better days, and I was rather counting on your old man coming across with the folding stuff, this being the way us princes do business when the chips are down. I am, after all, heir to the throne, and I do not fancy my chances if I turn up at my coronation attended by a couple of frogs. You know how it is with these fairy stories, there's always a few wicked uncles etcetera waiting behind the curtain for a chance to slip one over on the rightful heir. A scandal like this is all they need. Where's my hat?"

It was then that Cinderella's father interceded.

"But sire!" he cried. "My other daughters will bring with them a dowry of two million large ones in blue chip stock, plus several valuable freeholds and four gown factories!"

"That's more like it," said the Prince. "That would be the dames with the big feet, right?"

"Sadly, sire, yes."

"Sadly nothing!" snapped the Prince. "What's a pair of size nines when two people love each other?"

The father clapped his hands for joy, and the Ugly Sisters danced a little jig.

"And which of them shall it be, sire," cried their father,
"upon whom your royal fancy has fallen?"

"You got a coin?" said the Prince.

* * *

La Belle Dame Sans Argent

"O what can ail thee, knight-at-arms,
Alone and palely loitering?
The sedge has withered from the lake,
And no birds sing.

"O what can ail thee, knight-at-arms!
So haggard, and so woe-begone?
The squirrel's granary is full,
And the harvest's done."

"I'm glad you brought the squirrel up,
He's laughing, now his nuts have come;
Nice hole, warm leaves, security—
All right for some!

"I met a lady in the meads,
Full beautiful—a faery's child,
I thought 'If only she were <u>rich</u>!'
And then she smiled.

"Her teeth were 18-carat gold!
And there were emeralds in her hair!
And on her elfin finger shone
A solitaire!

"Mine was present at the birth, too. And that's the last I saw of him."

"I set her on my pacing steed,
(I've never liked the errant life,
Most knights are after just one thing—
A loaded wife).

"She took me to her elfin grot,
If grot's the word—6 bath, 9 bed,
Plus fourteen acres, and a lake—
This dame had <u>bread</u>!

"And there she lulled me asleep,
And there I dream'd—Ah! woe betide!
The latest dream I ever dream'd
On the cold hill's side.

"I saw solicitors, and tax
Advisers, and accountants, too:
They cried—'It's all in trust! Tied up!
It's not for you!'

"I saw their starv'd lips in the gloam
With horrid warning gapèd wide,
And I awoke and found me here
On the cold hill's side.

*"I'd withhold my favours if I could
remember what they were!"*

"And this is why I sojourn here
Alone and palely loitering,
Though the sedge is wither'd from the lake,
And no birds sing."

*   *   *

Enter, to the tomb, ROMEO, with lanthorn, crow and spade

ROMEO: Ah, dear Juliet,
Why art thou yet so fair? Shall I believe
That unsubstantial Death is amorous,
And that the lean abhorred monster keeps
Thee here in dark to be his paramour?
So much for slush. The thing is, where's the will?
Dear God, to think I nearly had it all!
One half Verona mine, as Montague,
The other chunk (did ever man play cards
More closely to his chest?) would come with thee!
Or, rather, did—for were we, after all,
Not spliced last night? Now look at you!
Stone cold, and, worse, intestate—there's the rub!
Here are my lawyers, Lanthorn, Crow & Spade,
And not one scrap of paper can we find!
No will, no deed of gift, no marriage bond,
And you can bet the bloody Capulets
Will fight this out in every lousy court
From here to Rome! Ah, stars, I had such plans!
New roads, new shopping precincts, tower blocks,
Hotels, convention centres, monorails
From here to Venice (which I would have drained
And made an Adriatic Disneyland);
But now? A plague on both our houses falls!
I would snatch up this poison, drain it down,
If I had not more sense.

Exeunt, oathing.

*   *   *

. . . Mellors paused at his intertwining, and the forget-me-nots dropped from his stricken fingers.

"Tha *what*?" he cried.

Constance Chatterley raised herself on one pink elbow, spilling cowslips, ragwort, poppies, geraniums, hollyhocks, and old man's beard.

"I said I've left him!" she exclaimed. "What care I for the mills and the factories, the mansions and the millions! As long as Lady Jane can have John Thomas, what more does she need?"

41

"Tha daft booger!" muttered the gamekeeper. "'Appen tha knows ah'll 'ave ter give oop nice little noomber 'ere, three quid a wik all found, cottage wi' tiled outhouse, own ferret, plus all the pheasants and salmon ah can lay 'ands on—what did tha want ter go and do a silly bloody thing like that fer?"

"Does John Thomas want more than Lady Jane?" simpered Constance Chatterley.

"It's all right for 'im, 'e dona need three squerr meals a day," said Mellors bitterly. "Tha'll be wantin' ter get dressed now, ah reckon."

"I shall be going to London on the night train," she said. "When will you join me?"

"Doan 'old tha breath," snapped Mellors. "Ah've 'eard tell where old Sir Reginald Furze-Maudley is 'avin trouble wi' 'is waterworks—Leddy Furze-Maudley can't be more'n forty, and got more firm flesh on'er than a prize gammon-sow, hee, hee, hee! They just bought one o' they 'orseless kerridges, they'll be needin' a driver, ah reckon. Ah allus wanted ter drive a 'orseless kerridge, big gaiters, shiny 'at, brass buttons, and Leddy Furze-Whatsit gittin' randy on t'back seat—*and shut the bloody gate!*" he shouted.

"Never 'ad no manners, that one," muttered Mellors, to himself.

"It goes back quite a few years—they started a women's liberation movement or something."

"Well, shall we lure him on the rocks or shan't we?"

Fiona MacCarthy on

THE WOMANLY WEEKEND

I LIKE the thought of week-ends. Oh, the lovely stretch of leisure: leisure for boating and for gentle walks and picnicking; leisure for croquet and strawberries and cream; time to take the boy to sail a boat on the Round Pond or to see the Toy Museum or to look at Harrods Zoo and the other nice diversions they suggest for idle infants in the Sunday papers and the glossy magazines. I have pretty little visions of our weekend's entertaining: smart amusing people in for Cointreau on the Rocks, and men in gorgeous tunics lounging in on Sunday morning for the meal which the Cookery Editors call Brunch. Time for the life as it is lived in Colour Supplements: this is what I hope for from weekend to weekend.

But weekends aren't like that. Not the weekends I am used to. From the moment when I wake up on a Saturday, too early, aroused by grunts and creakings which mean my child is managing to climb out of his cot and will soon land at my bedside and triumphantly shout "Mummy," I know that my weekend, as usual, is doomed. As I dress and wash the boy and make the bed and grill the bacon, I realise that weekends were not really built for women. A weekend, I keep finding, is just one of those illusions. It's a man's life or a child's life: it is no fun for a wife.

A weekend, for a child, is a fine time for self-expression. Time for getting muddy; time for tearing clothes; time for getting paints out to decorate the wall; time for asking friends in, so one has a little army of boys with carts and tricycles for churning up the lawn. Weekends are ice-cream time and iced-lolly time and crisp time. At weekends there is very little children's television: maybe "Pogles Wood" and Dougal are a kind of childish safety valve. At any rate, the riots in our house increase on Sundays. And as for the idea of taking children to museums: my child had such hysterics in the V & A that a keeper, quite a kind one, said I perhaps would be wiser not to bring him there again.

Men, I find, at weekends are just as uncontrollable, in more subtle, much more esoteric ways. They have secret plans, precluding them from helping with the shopping, or hanging out the washing, or finishing the dishes, cleaning shoes or mending fuses or any of the other admittedly most dreary jobs you hoped that they might do. The reassuring notion that marriage is a partnership tends, I think, to fall apart completely at weekends. For men lead their own lives—drinking lives or sporting lives, gardening lives, building lives or even paper-reading lives—which somehow they put over as essential, even noble. At weekends, men are living on a rather higher plane.

The scope for self-expression at weekends for a woman is in fact extremely limited, one might say non-existent. The traditional activities at weekends are all manly. When a woman comes along she is simply an appendage. Women at a cricket match; women motor-racing; women punting down the Cherwell on a sunny afternoon; women in restaurants, in pubs or out at dances: a woman is an oddity, one feels, without a man. Even modern occupations, like raves and late, late movies and ICA excitements and the Saturday Night Bowl, somehow feel a bit unnatural for solitary females. That's the thing about the weekend; it looks better with a man.

Not that married women are intent on self-expression. At the weekends, with a family, there simply isn't time. That lovely stretch of leisure is a desperate succession of little tasks and big tasks and providing cups of tea. Little tasks like shopping lists and sewing on the buttons and flicking through the papers to see what one is missing; enormous tasks like lugging home three basketsful of vegetables. The physical labour of weekends is quite astounding. Far from serving Cointreau on the Rocks to sparkling people, for heaven's sake, I'm on my knees and scrubbing out the cupboards. Instead of cooking Brunch food—mounds of Scrambled Egg with Garlic—I am in my husband's workshop carting planks of wood about.

The main point I am making is not simply that a weekend is a snare and a delusion (although of course it is), but that weekends have a strange effect on individual women. Look at them: at weekends they are almost all the same, making coffee, packing sandwiches, plastering up grazes, cleaning boots and washing nappies, trying to keep cheerful in the face of a family which more or less ignores them as they scurry through the house. Whatever they are like through the week—well-paid executives, dreamy house-bound mothers, secretaries, actresses—a weekend

will reduce them to a dismal kind of sameness. As we quick-roast Sunday chickens, we are nearly all alike.

I have my own small theory. (I need a little theory to keep me reasonably sane through each weekend.) The theory is that weekends and the week-long build up are simply the invention of self-preserving man. It's all a plot, the weekend food and clothes and fun and glamour. The weekend is the time when women are done down. Why not admit that week-ends are just masculine devices (in Britain anyway) for giving men the upper hand?

"Oh, for heaven's sake, Granny—you can't expect boxing every night."

Lines to Status

ANGELA MILNE

SPIRIT of all that's new and costs a pile,
   Haunter of what we read and where we shop;
Guider round neighbours' houses, with a smile;
   Lord of a language full of words like Top
And Trend; bright demon, stay away from us
Women who've opted out of all that fuss.

We are no target for your whispering:
   Still got that cooker? Tablecloths like those?
Have we seen Mrs. S's bedside thing?
   Why aren't our curtains done like Mrs. O's?
Why don't we buy a Spanish soup-bowl set?
Haven't we got a bathroom carpet yet?

Spirit, you waste your time. We've heard it all;
   Are well aware what central heating is,
How plastic tiles take backache from the hall,
   How second cars are musts for families,
Even how swimming-pools are made, and how
One can buy garden-rooms in sections now—

So hop it. Leave us with our egg-whisks, which
   Are Woolworth's bent; our sides-to-middle sheets.
We do not need you, demon; we are rich
   Although we never trod your gilt-paved streets.
Our assets are intangibles and worth
More than all yours. Indeed we own the earth.

Knowing the joy of life, the golden ties
   Of love and friendship, and the zeal of health,
Cherishing to the soul that matchless prize
   Of womanhood, the one true source of wealth
(Besides the cause of our financial state):
Our children: beautiful and strong and straight—

What's that we hear you snarling? *"Silly fools!*
   When now with all that social welfare rot,
Doctors and orange juice and teeth and schools,
   Experts, advisers, visitors, the lot,
Such assets are what anyone can own.
Things that count to-day are mine alone."

Do You Take This Woman to be Your Executive Assistant . . .?

The Institute of Directors is planning advice to young executives on choosing wives. Including the all-important interview?

MILES KINGTON reports

A penthouse flat. Soft lights. Soft furniture. A sofa. On it, the young executive and the girl of his dreams.

Executive: Comfortable?

Girl: Mmm.

Executive: Drink all right?

Girl: Fine.

Executive: OK, let's get down to business. I'll put a record on.

Girl: Super. Have you got the latest by . . .?

Executive: Just a moment. Let *me* ask the questions. I have here in my hand three LPs, one by Schubert, one by Dave Brubeck and one by the Rolling Stones. Which one do you choose?

Girl: Well, I don't really like any . . . oh, Brubeck will do.

Executive: Brubeck. *(He makes a note in a notebook.)* I wouldn't say that showed a high degree of social awareness, would you, Diana?

Girl: What do you mean, social awareness?

Executive: *(Raises his eyebrows and makes another note. He switches the gramophone on.)* How do you like my place?

Girl: Very much. It's very . . . nice.

Executive: If you lived here, what changes would you make?

Girl: Ah, that's different. If it was mine, I'd take down those hideous curtains, which are too short anyway; I'd move the desk, which blocks the window; I'd get rid of these silly cushions, rearrange the lighting, switch the sofa over there . . .

Executive *(busy writing)* Thats very significant.

Girl: What is?

Executive: I said, "if you *lived* here". You said, "if the place was *mine*".

Girl: Well, darling, you know.

Executive: Diana, I want to ask you a very important question.

Girl: *(shyly)* Yes?

Executive: What do you think of marriage?

Girl: Is this a proposal?

Executive: No, it's a motivation research inquiry.

Girl: Oh. Well, I don't want to seem fuddy-duddy, but I still think it's rather a sacred thing, very much for better or worse . . .

Executive: No, no, I mean do you think marriage is still a viable proposition? And if so, do you see it as basically an economic move, a pooling of productive resources or simply a public relations exercise? You should quote statistics where-ever relevant.

Girl: I don't know what you're talking about!

Executive: Do you see that mark on the coffee table? What does it remind you of?

Girl: A coffee stain. Jim, what is this all . . .

Executive: *(Admiringly)* You do show a refreshing ability to reach the heart of a problem. Well, for example, would you rather have two children or five?

Girl: Two. No, five!

Executive: *(writing busily)* "Is equally aware of advantages of high quality output and mass production." How would you see your role as a partner to a male executive, marriage-wise?

Girl: Let *me* ask a question. Why, when I asked for a Brubeck record, did you put on Frank Sinatra?

Executive: Because it's company policy. *(Turns a page.)* "A healthy instinct to question company policy." So you see marriage as a long-term, non-renewable contract, do you?

Girl: If you want to put it like that—yes.

Executive: Then, Diana, I have only one more question to ask. *(He goes down on one knee.)* Darling, will you accept a post as executive wife to me, subject to the usual physical examination and reference inquiries?

Girl: What do you mean—physical examination?

Executive: *(Attempting to lead her to the bedroom)* Well, your appointment would take effect from the 23rd January at St. John's Church, but there would have to be a short trial period. Your salary would be at least £1,500, plus use of my car . . .

Girl: Let me go! Let me go! I think you've gone mad!

Executive: But you don't understand. I'm offering you the job!

Girl: *(Crying, grabbing her coat)* I don't know what you're talking about and I don't want to see you ever again! Now let me out of here!

Executive: It's Frank Dunlop, isn't it?

Girl: What's Frank got to do with it?

Executive: Oh, I know all about you and Frank. You pretend to be interested in me, but deep down it's Frank. How much has he offered you? £2,000 a year? More?

Girl: You just don't understand, do you? Goodbye, Jim! *(She rushes out.)*

Executive: *(Clasps head for a moment, then starts writing)* "The candidate was in many ways suitable for the post, but showed little sign of being able to sublimate her ambition to company requirements. Nevertheless, I am still desperately in love with her . . ." *(He stares into space for a moment, crosses this out and continues.)* "Nevertheless I feel sure that if the Institute of Directors were to put in a good word for me . . ."

"Here he is and he doesn't look too happy . . .

"Let's see now . . . they lost! . . . they were thrashed! Four-nil? No. FIVE-NIL?"

"George, your face is a picture. Don't ever try to hide anything from me, love."

POSEUSE

Some rather smart occupations for rather smart girls. *MONICA FURLONG*

THERE is only a handful of really chic openings for girls and as for some reason these are never on the books of employment agencies, still less on the lips of headmistresses, I am taking the trouble to rehearse them for the benefit of those leaving school this summer.

Women War Correspondents. There is only moderate employment in this field at the moment, but it is a peach of a job if you can land it. "A gallant, indomitable little figure" (learn that phrase by heart, it's bound to come in useful), you will win the admiration of all. Worshipped by the men, revered by the officers, respected by the general, feared by the Prime Minister, loved by all, you will probably get a decoration (as well as perks in the way of memoir-writing later on). "For fearless courage," runs the citation, "not only in the face of the enemy but also under great provocation from our own side. She never wavered." Useful qualifications for this post are: an aureole of red-gold hair (preferably naturally curly—those fox-holes are *damp*), a tip-tilted freckled little nose, and of course a gallant, indomitable little figure, well propped up by gallant, indomitable little legs. And it might be as well to have a gallant, indomitable little editor somewhere in the background to make sense of your rapturous communiqués.

But for most of us it's no use dreaming of battlefields, however Elysian, so let's be severely practical. What about becoming the mother of eight? Six will do if you're a writer as well (it seems amazing that you should be practical enough to conceive at all). If you happen also to be in society, this is quite certainly your gimmick. I guarantee that not once will your name appear in "London Last Night" without reference to your remarkable obstetric virtuosity. It is nice for the children too because they grow up quite without fear of crowds and are never happier than in the Tube in the rush-hour. A charming touch if your husband is a cricketer is to have one or two extra children for luck, so that he can crack to the reporter "Ha! A cricket team, what?" I cannot recommend a Rugby Union husband, however, as one must eschew ostentation. Marriage is a useful, though not absolutely essential qualification for this particular profession, and a nice, motherly smile will help you to conceal minor thorns in the flesh, such as an obsessive dislike of small children.

If, however, Dick-Read is not your favourite bedside reading we must think again. There are always openings for invalids, or more precisely, ex-invalids. You know, people who overcome things. Mrs. McNamara was told she would never walk again, and now look at her pedalling briskly to her work as a Cantilever Charge-hand. "You will never play the ocarina again," doctors told Lilian Crosby of Balham, but Lily and her mother just would not give up. Two years later Lily played the ocarina at the Albert Hall before the Queen Mother, watched by the faithful physiotherapist who had made her dreams come true. You see the possibilities? The snag about this job is that you must have something to overcome in the first place, and self-mutilation with pecuniary intent never quite fills the bill, I'm afraid.

Girls with titles will find any of the following pleasant jobs to hold down: eloping (a bit hackneyed this), getting engaged without parents' knowledge or consent to somebody quite impossible, breaking off engagement to somebody highly possible, being frightfully nice to Old Age Pensioners.

An interesting occupation for girls, though I have not yet completed my routine probe into qualifications and working conditions, is vampirism, and this they tell me shows signs of a boom in popularity. So my advice is—jump in quickly with both fangs while the going is good. If this work attracts you but you have not the confidence or experience to become a fully-qualified vampire, why not join the National Blood Transfusion Service? This is very satisfying work.

Really young girls with a talent for scribbling cannot do better than to have a thoroughly wretched love-life and drive furiously about the country damaging expensive cars. This is an occupation which has my full recommendation, as has being an infant prodigy. If you are lucky enough to have been systematically starved during your formative years (and parents are not always as careful about this as they might be) you will have a good chance in modelling, but I must warn you that you are wasting your time unless your shoulder-blades and collar-bones are sharp enough to cut a glossy sheet of paper clean in two.

A blissful ploy for the small woman is to be the wan, downtrodden wife of a famous, handsome man—say an actor or a bishop renowned for his melting pulpit manner. "Poor thing," the gratifying whisper will follow you, "I bet he doesn't waste much of his famous charm on *her*." Or "Charity begins at home, I *don't* think." A similar but rather strenuous employment is to marry a boring young twig on the margin of contemporary affairs—a Conservative back-bencher, say—and briskly wriggle him to the Front Bench. "Where would he be without *her*, I should like to know?" "Power behind the throne, eh?" "She's got a good head on her shoulders, that girl." All pretty good fun.

These are just a few tentative suggestions. Of course if you are a mousy, unenterprising little thing you could always try work.

MY NEXT HUSBAND

BARBARA CASTLE

MY next husband will definitely be hen-pecked. Everyone laughably assumes my present one is so I may as well have the advantage of exchanging illusion for reality.

This means he will be able to mend a fuse. Being good about the house is the essential ingredient of the manageable male. All these pretensions to having green fingers as an excuse for spending the morning in the sunshine and tramping in from the garden in muddy boots are really no substitute.

As a career woman, who earns her living serving up solutions on all the insoluble problems from the balance of payments to Bangladésh, it has always been my dream to be married to a handyman. Women whose husbands are relaxed about rawlplugs don't know what worry is. I would sleep peacefully at night with anyone who could tell a pair of pincers from a wire cutter. Apart from the blissful convenience, I could really at last begin to live it up.

If you are buried in the depths of the country as I like to be whenever I can, it costs you a fiver just to have a bolt put on the shed door or to bribe the nearest plumber to come and look at a dripping tap. I calculate I could have a trip to the Solomon Islands every year out of the money we will save on the washers my new do-it-yourself paragon will whip off and on our taps.

My next husband will not say every time I get out the travel brochures: "I do love England in the summer: don't you think it would be nice to holiday at home? The garden is at its best then." I know what that means: staying up half the night cutting up his glut of runner beans for the deep freeze.

It means more time for him to indulge his passion for growing shallots and Jerusalem artichokes—and then complain when he doesn't get them at every meal. I have lost more honest housekeepers scraping artichokes and chopping shallots than Ted Heath has broken election promises.

My paragon will also find it possible to go into our local pub without ordering a cartload of manure from our farmer friend. I could then spend Easter as it should be spent —admiring the daffodils—instead of being driven out of bed to do the muck-spreading.

Being the submissive type, my next husband would not feel that being married to an MP meant that he had to recite the Declaration of Independence over every detail of our married life. He would not snort: "Of course I don't need a shopping list. I am not a fool." And then forget to buy the bread. He would not go sternly round the house reprimanding everyone else for leaving on lights and then find the car lights he had left on all night had given us a flat battery just when I needed to be rushed up to London for a Three-Line Whip. He would never, never make that elementary masculine mistake of equating life and liberty with the pursuit of snappiness.

Being a handyman he would, of course, be an expert cook. It would be he who would rustle up the omelette at midnight after a heavy day. And he would not believe that every cooking utensil within sight was expendable. I would never again have to curse the friend who once told us that the only way to do steak was in a totally dry, red-hot frying pan with a dash of Lea & Perrins to add piquancy. I like charcoaled steak as much as anyone but it comes expensive when it means charcoaling the entire kitchen too. I shall relinquish without regret the record I at present hold of being married to the only man in Britain who has ever managed to burn a boiled egg.

In what kind of profession shall I find my paragon? Certainly, I will never again marry a journalist. For an MP that is the simplest recipe for civil war since Charles I tried to arrest the leaders of the Parliamentarians. I don't mind those Cavalier Fleet Street chaps who prop up El Vino's bar every lunchtime keeping abreast of current affairs, i.e. gossiping about the latest scandal in the newspaper industry.

"Don't just stand there, help me find the oven. Your supper's in it."

"Talk to you? Why? Am I supposed to be Kenneth Harris?"

(NB Women's Lib: do they still forbid women to go into El Vino's unless they sit down meekly in the inside room?) I don't even mind—in fact, I rather like—the current cult of exuberant side-whiskers for which my present husband is undoubtedly responsible.

But I do object when they set up to be Cromwellians, too, telling the politicians how to run Parliament and trampling over their egos on every comment page. (If anyone tramples on *their* egos, they promptly send for a solicitor.) The trouble with journalists is that they are always calling on politicians to "communicate". That is bad enough in the public field. What it means is that the only thing a politician can get into the news is the one thing he thought he had a right to keep to himself—such as whether he likes HP sauce with his meals, for instance, or snores in bed. But it really is too much to carry this running war into the bosom of the family. Who wants the New Model Army camping out in their own home?

After long and mature consideration I have come to the conclusion that the next man I marry will be a hairdresser. Any husband who cannot back-comb his wife's hair is not worth his salt. This will mean that I shall be able to go into every serious TV discussion completely light-heartedly. It won't matter a damn what I talk about. My friends will all ring up to remark: "Saw you on TV last night. Your hair did look nice".

Let Me Through!
I'm a Pressure Group!

IN our buildings were twelve blocks, each stone of stair, tiled of wall and defective landing lights; each graced by the same stroke of flamboyance in that a tile trim had been introduced, employing the use of three distinctive colours; blue, green and brown. Thus, four blocks had the blue trim, four green and four brown. If you lived in a green block you would have a natural affinity for those who also lived in a green block. Your fellow green blocker might be a beast, a bully, a thief, an eater of neat Oxo cubes, a pee-er in bicycle sheds, even a catholic, yet he remained, inescapably, one of your own. While a blue or brown blocker might be sheer heaven and buy you lolly-ices after Saturday morning pictures, there would still be this ineradicable shadow between you. It depended on the colour of home ground. Or, if you prefer, on where you stood.

It was, you might say, chauvinism in embryo, the whole filthy, prejudicial mess whining through infancy. But it happens, like the Way Things Are, to be true as it is indefensible and I only mention it at all because I feel I have a fight on my hands. The trouble is, I find it impossible to define the difference between inside and outside, establishment and disestablishment, status quo and pressure group without saying that it depends on where you stand (or in some cases on where you sit).

Is the status quo a monster steam-roller, ironing out folk too frail to climb aboard or nip out of its path? Or a sort of noble artefact, crumbling gently beneath subversives as they befoul it like a swarm of rogue blow-flies? Or is it a pillar, made entirely of other pillars? And if so, are you a pillar or is the pillar standing on your foot? So what if you don't like it standing on your foot? Might you not scrawl a rude word or two upon its cool surface, or kick it with your free foot and fall flat on your bum? Then, as you struggle ruefully to regain your one-footed posture at the plinth, might you not wonder who thumped who?

Pressure, I think we can fairly assume, is that which knocks you out of kilter. A pressure group, on the other hand, tends to do nothing of the kind. It is single or plural, specialized or generalized and means he, she or it who seeks to get his, her or its own way. It is that which thinks it knows best and seeks to enjoin others to its ranks. It is even that which seeks to go about its business without being crushed, diverted or mucked about. All of which brings me to the conclusion that the ultimate pressure group is the status quo, while that which we, in our quest for expediency and security, describe as a pressure group is a mere smoke-screen for the pillar of pillars. What we call a pressure group, in fact, is more accurately defined as a de-pressure, or vacuum group.

I, all alone, am a vacuum group. That is to say I defend myself against those who urge me to grow up, get married, have babies, curtsey to the Queen, kneel to the Lord, vote Conservative, paint the front of my house, have my cats neutered, buy a new one rather than get it mended, stop trying to be funny, be successful or give up. I ally myself with other vacuum groups which I recognize from their impotent and defensive natures.

"What did you do for social equality?" our scruffy grandchildren will ask. "I swilled a bottle of beer as the Queen smiled by," we reply. "What did you do for Biafra?"—"I knocked a policeman's helmet off." "What did you do for Women's Liberation?"—"I said fuck on television." We'll take a pride in having neither passed a law, made a profit nor shared a ham roll with Mary Whitehouse in the BBC canteen.

Ah, but it's a lonely row to hoe. Which is probably why vacuum groupers go in for meetings although finding out where they might be is not an easy thing to do. Take public enemy number one, the Anarchists. I know they exist, you know they exist, Mr. Carr knows they exist. But where? I've tried, God knows I've tried to rub shoulders. I've been in and out of the Old Bailey more times than a recidivist, poking bags of apples and earnest questionnaires through cell bars, making appointments and promising space in above-ground publications. And all for nothing. In the end all I was sure of was a couple of them had pinched a cheque book and felt rather bad about it.

Then there's Gay Liberation. They're good fun at somebody's rally, but left to their own devices all they do is sit about asking each other for rather spurious reassurances, just like Young Conservatives. "Excuse me, I'm gay and Jewish, is that all right?"—"Well, I'm a gay Buddhist and I don't have any trouble"—"What about me, I'm a gay postman, should I come out with the others next Tuesday?" All about as staggering as the Women's Liberation meeting I attended in trendy New York when two hundred ladies were perplexed by the question "How do you *know* if you've had an orgasm?"

We rattle our wheelchairs and rustle our pension books in the strangers' gallery, we dress our children up in placards demanding they should be removed from out of sight at public expense, we march and sit, sit and march, and we never do any harm. Our problem is we don't know how to. We're too simple, too concerned with injustice as opposed to justice, too straightforward, too responsive. We do not grasp the finer points of manipulative behaviour. Brain-washing, which is what you have to be clever at in order to get anything changed, is a psychopathic exercise perfected by only the most cunning, as anyone who has ever been in a Chinese prison will tell you. Or anyone who's been in the Brownies, come to that, but more of that to follow.

My first experience of such devilishness was indirect but nonetheless affecting. The victim was my little brother, an impressionable soul whose eyes behind their chipped spectacles held promise of a sweet and gullible nature. Something terrible happened to him when he first went to school; I know it was shocking because my mother used to lower her voice when she spoke of it. A nun, it would appear, had given him something to hold in bed. Our mummy went all pinched round the nostrils when she found it there, clutched in his obedient fist, and I knew when she sobbed to my father, "They *swore* they wouldn't do anything like this" that our family had come under the most violent pressure. The little silver medal thing, bearing the image of who knows what figure of saintliness, was returned to the Oratory with a curt note, but I'm sure we won the day. I often wonder what effect this scandalous indoctrination had on my hitherto innocent sibling, and whether it relates to the fact he rapidly turned into one of those easily-led buffoons who ends up a prince of commerce driving about in a Bentley.

Nothing nearly so crushing happened to me until much later. True, they brought me up on Truby King and I still can't go wee-wee lying down, but I don't grumble about that often. Anyway, it was me who insisted I join the Brownies. They dressed me up like a proper little soldier girl in a tiny battledress with a tie and a tiepin appropriately depicting a stick-insect writhing on a bar and sent me off to the church hall on Friday evenings. What happened to us all in the prefabricated dust trap would make a Maoist recruiting drive look like a fourth form tea-dance.

The intention of Brown Owl and her cronie, Tawny Owl, was to rob all us little girls of our identities, then further confuse us by making us say incomprehensible things which were totally unrelated to what we were actually doing until our minds were clear for further bending on account of we had been driven out of them.

To be enrolled was to be deprived of human status and turned into a gnome, elf, pixie or fairy. At meetings we were obliged to emit strange chants to this effect. We're the fairies here's our aim, lend a hand and play the game. Here you see the jolly pixies, helping people out of fixes. We are what are called the elves, do for others not ourselves. Our next discipline was to queue up and do penny-six to Brown Owl, who made ticks and crosses in her book according to how our fairy-selves measured up to her concept of excellence. The penny was a simple penny which might or might not have gone towards Brown Owl's travelling expenses, and no harm in that. But the six was for certain objects you had to have about your person, such as string, sling for broken arm, pencil, penknife, notebook—none of which insidiously enough, were ever in fact employed. Should you fail with one of these possessions, you were marked penny-five—and so on down to the disgrace of penny-nothing. Our chantings grew more mysterious as the evening wore on. There was a lot of stuff about doing our duty to goddannaking, plus jigging round flags and imaginary toadstools. All we actually *did*, in terms of direct, non-dogmatic action, was take our shoes off and skid about the floor touching walls and return to line.

We were being osmotically trained to enjoy life at the bottom, from whence we would come to judge our rightful place in the Establishment. We imagined, not unreasonably, that Brown Owl could get to Princess Elizabeth and Lady Baden-Powell, whose photographs in mahogany frames decorated our headquarters, and do her penny-sixes to them. But she was as high up the ladder as we could see; for the time being we could toady to her alone. Hence we would fight to first blood for the job of pumping up her tyres or carrying her hold-all across the church-yard.

It was soon after I declined the latter favour that I was drummed out of the Brownies. I was, Brown Owl told my mother, a bad influence on the other girls, a complaint she failed to enlarge upon except to say I was rebellious. Her perception was nothing if not sensory and bully for her, she knew where she stood.

"I said I'd let you out for an hour to get married . . . there was no mention of bridesmaids!"

THE FIRST MINK

by
Graham

*"Darling, **please** stop going on about all these poor little animals."*

"I thought it seemed a little chilly in here."

"Oh, for heaven's sake!"

"Come to bed, Adele!"

"Damn! Another mild sunny day!"

61

The First Two Weeks are the Worst

Survive the honeymoon, reports ANN LESLIE, and your marriage can survive anything.

I'M told that along the rainswept pierheads of English summer-seasons, the damp souls of comics are still sprouting honeymoon stories, knowing that a joke about newly-weds has the effect of instantly galvanising old ladies in deck-chairs—like hitting them on the knee with a hammer. "No, see, eh?, no, don't laugh, there was this honeymoon couple see . . . ooooh, *naughty*, I can see you darlin', put 'im *down* . . . anyway, this honeymoon couple . . ." Nudge, nudge, ho, ho. Maeve and Else cackle joyously through their toffomints remembering how Fred's mates at the bottle-works put frogs in Alice's wedding bed and gave her such a turn. In those days, honeymoons were epic events in one's life, something worthy of being laughed at . . .

Mind you, it was always working-class honeymoons which were supposed to be ipso facto screamingly funny: never upper-class ones. Working class honeymoons were spent in boarding houses with noisy bed-springs which rang out like tocsins across the prom. Upper class ones were apparently always Romantic, spent by limp-wristed young things called Charles and Amanda at Cap d'Antibes, surrounded by champagne buckets and portly Hungarians playing passionate fiddles under the trees. Curiously, sex didn't seem to come into the latter sort of honeymoon at all, whereas in the first type, it was the only thing that did.

But on the whole it looks as if the honeymoon joke is gradually losing its place in the joke-book pantheon, along with all those other sure-fire rib-ticklers, Scotsmen, sporrans, mother-in-law and public loos. Permissiveness has probably killed it off.

After all, the whole point of the honeymoon joke was that it was the First Time they'd Had It. Now, by all accounts, everyone's Had It almost as soon as they've cut their milk teeth.

I remember being told by one world-weary little thirteen year old in California, how much she deplored the declining moral standards of today's eight year olds. "Sex, sex, sex, that's all they ever think of. Why, when I was their age I was still playing with dolls" she said, as she popped Tuesday's pill out of its easy-dial packet and set off for another hair-bleaching session at the beauty salon.

Now *I* was brought up—ah, what innocent aeons ago—by nuns who told their spotty little charges that a man who Truly Loved you would Respect you until the wedding night, whereupon, apparently, appalling disrespect would take place, which was unfortunately the price you had to pay for the privilege of frying his fish-fingers and soaking his smalls for the rest of your days.

We heard a great deal about woman's Finer Feelings and man's Lower Instincts but never had a chance to put the theories to the test since the only males for miles around our convent were Ron, the scrofulous gardeners boy—and gloomy Father Flaherty, the parish priest, fresh from the bog, with a face like a fist, a hot line in hellfire, and a habit of tying his gloves to his wrists in case he lost them, so that during his passionate sermons on Fleshy Lust, they bobbed and weaved hysterically about his body like giant bees . . .

But nowadays of course it's all different and the whole sexual initiation part of a honeymoon has gone. Now the honeymoon is meant to be nothing less than a divine, star-spun interlude for you both before you get down to the real nitty-gritty of life among the Squeezy mops in Spanland.

Of course, you're still supposed to spend most of it joyously tumbling about in bed together, only none of that beginner's stuff: it's got to be a really jazzy production number these days, real high-wire acrobatics. The whole thing imposes an intolerable strain on a couple who've only just managed to pull through the horrors of the wedding reception.

Most of my married friends swear they all came nearest to divorce during their honeymoons.

Like a girl-friend of mine who spent her wedding night tramping about Dawlish and district in the rain with a husband who said he swore he remembered the hotel they'd booked into was called Seaview, and for Christsake, stop moaning, there couldn't be more than twenty Seaviews in Dawlish, *could* there . . . Well, there could, and actually it was called Seacliffe, and by the time they got there Mrs. Potter said she was ever so sorry but she'd disposed of the Bridal Suite to a commercial traveller, and some hours later the bride barked coldly at her spouse as she boarded the coach home to mother "I'm having THIS annulled for a start!"

Surviving the honeymoon is probably the first great hurdle in a marriage. I was once despatched to Canada on a ship which, my editor was erroneously informed, was a Honeymoon Special, groaning at the gunwhales with 1,500 emigrating newly-weds.

In fact there were four. The first couple had inadvertently been booked into separate cabins by the steamship company:

she sharing with three Jehovah's Witnesses, and he with four members of a construction gang heading for Saskatchewan.

The other couple, who'd won their "dream" honeymoon in a cornflake contest, were together, but only just, as she spent most of the time being sick in the cabin while he glumly downed guinnesses and played shove ha'penny in the bar. Beneath us the wintry Atlantic heaved like a peptic whale. After a honeymoon like that, married life in Moose Jaw or Calgary could only be a blissful improvement . . .

Of course, the over-selling of honeymoons has even begun to worry social workers. One of them, the secretary of the Fulham and Hammersmith Citizens' Advice Bureau, no less, was recently quoted by the News of the World as blaming "honeymoon blues" for the break-up of so many young marriages. "The proceedings" she said "aren't as romantic as they would like them to be."

Well of course not. Honeymoons are a time for the destruction of illusions, particularly those appertaining to the naturally dewy-fresh beauty of the bride. Before marriage you could maintain your beauty was a gift from God and didn't come expensively bottled by Max Factor.

Many's the young husband who must have suffered a cold frisson of fright on first glimpsing his wife minus eyebrows and eyelashes and all greased up like a Channel swimmer in Orange Skin Food. Of course, in America they've already thought of that, and the bride can buy sex-prufe lipstick, eyelashes and wigs, and in case you've got the sort of droopy boobs which hit your knees with a thud when you shed your bra, you can buy nightdresses with built-in foundation garments: "So soft, so subtle. He'll never Guess!"

To keep the illusion going, you can also book into that

"Care to break training?"

ultimate sexual depressant, the Honeymoon hotel, complete with heart-shaped bed, heart-shaped bath, heart-shaped swimming pool, heart-shaped skating rink, and heart-shaped jokes pinned over the dining room exits saying "We know where you're going!" Over the beds, there's a heart-shaped mirror so you can watch yourself in action, if, that is, you've got the heart for it any more...

The only honeymoon I've had so far doesn't encourage me to try another. Ever. We were married in Compton and squabbled furiously all the way down to our hotel in Midhurst.

On arrival, my husband, who puts his all into rows and consequently finds them very debilitating, sank exhausted with rage onto the fourposter and fell asleep, while I went downstairs and watched James Mason in "Five Fingers" on the hotel telly. Actually this was rather appropriate as I'd been in love with Mason for years and had always dreamt, while doodling on my Latin Primer, of spending my wedding night with James anyway. I once wrote him a poem in which I described his voice as "soft footfalls in the dark" which I thought amazingly good, but which inexplicably failed to bring him panting to my side. My husband had always felt the same way about Anne Bancroft, but well, there you are. James and Anne always seemed to be otherwise occupied, so we'd had to settle for each other instead.

The next day we flew to Switzerland to ski, where I promptly broke my leg, due to being hit by a tree which sprang out of the ski-slope, narrowly missing my husband but pole-axeing me. It probably knew I was on honeymoon. By then suffering from honeymooner's paranoia, I felt sure I heard it rattling its cones with sadistic glee as I passed out in a red haze at its feet.

I spent the rest of our honeymoon—all ten days of it—in a plaster-cast lying on a playdeck half way up an Alp wedged between motionless rows of old ladies wrapped in blankets mummifying in the sun, with plastic "beaks" sprouting from their sunglasses to save their noses from peeling. They resembled a lot of up-ended owls and none of them were great conversationalists—except for the lady who told me every day that she could forecast avalanches by the excruciating twinges she got in her lower intestine, and her friend, who apparently owned three-quarters of Peru and had an understandable thing about Communists.

After three days of this, the sight of my husband, bronzed, merry, magnificent, shussing down the mountainside surrounded by gaily carolling girls made me long to shove him down a crevasse, hobble home and collect on the life insurance.

Things are improving now, but the honeymoon scars took some time to heal and I can't say I've ever quite forgiven him yet...

A Secretary is Not a Toy

ALAN BRIEN looks at sex in the office

IN 21 years of journalism, I have never had a secretary. I realise the ambiguity of that confession—urgh, urgh, gloat, gloat, know what I mean? If I go on to say that the most I have ever had has been a part of a secretary, I sink even deeper into a morass of *double-entendres*.

It seems almost impossible for a man to talk about secretaries without conjuring up the vision of a sort of Bunny-Office, with short-skirted poppets leaning slightly too far over desks, holding notepads where "X" marks the spot on exposed thighs, squatting with careless provacation by filing cabinets, packing dirty-weekend kits into executive briefcases with many a knowing look and booking hotel rooms.

What was once the description of the wife-mother-mistress-nanny - chauffeur - cook - confidant - time keeper - accountant-drinking companion - games partner - bodyguard - babysitter — has now become the specification for the secretary. She has the added advantage, in male fantasy, of being the consort who is hired by the week, the girl Friday who can be fired next Monday without any fuss about alimony, the status symbol which is always replaceable from stock, or the boardroom toy which is expendable, when the batteries run out, by standing order from manufacturers who are working on the New! Improved! Secret Formula! model. And what's more, or rather less, the secretary does not have to be charged against your account. The firm will pay.

The wife complains that the husband treats the home like an office. That the unknown caller on the telephone is always more intriguing than the too-well-known listener by the television. That he examines his folders of work with more interest than her carriers of shopping. That his interlude there is regarded as just a toll-gate which must be passed through on his way back to the real life of business. And the office is treated like a home, a home where man is the genuine boss, where children have their proper places as a group photograph on the desk, where the young close the door when they leave the room and speak only when they are spoken to on the intercom, where no one expects the boss figure to change dirty carbons, wash up the coffee cups, warm the whisky bottle or answer the door in his dressing gown.

The secretary is a Jeeves with curves, the slave of the press button, the genie with the light brown stare, a nubile Mary Poppins, Dr. Watson in drag, Dandini played by Cinderella. As a wife-substitute, having brought your coffee, sewed on your button, booked your holiday, doctored your hangover, told your lies, shown such devotion to your monologues that she takes them down in shorthand and embalms them in triplicate, what should be more natural and inevitable than that she should share your bed?

This view of secretaries, encouraged by clerical agencies with their coy, suggestive slogans and their posters showing queues of willing girl office workers all legs and no heads, is the masculine stereotype. The revelation by Xaviera Hollander, the Happy Hooker, that she was chosen Holland's Top Secretary in 1964 only confirms our deep-rooted belief that women only really go to work to meet us. The secretary has replaced the actress, the waitress, the barmaid, the shop girl, the air hostess, in male mythology, as a courtesan in training who vamps till ready on her typewriter.

It is, of course, just as far from reality as the ads which picture secretaries as spending their days jetting to Bangkok to order a couple of white elephants for a Hollywood epic, bandying epigrams with cabinet ministers, entering best-selling writers in nightclubs and picnicking beside the Rolls on Dordogne hillsides, about which the professional association of executive secretaries has been recently complaining. But such an illusion is hardly surprising when one of their own trade mags—*Top Secretary*—can show on its cover an elegant secretary with champagne glass in hand, perched on the director's desk, gazing with bemused delight at a chocolate, while the office butler awaits her permission to carry on pouring and the boss grins in happy admiration at the hieroglyphs in her notebook.

In Mary Kathleen Benét's book *Secretary—An Inquiry Into The Female Ghetto* (undoubtedly the most intelligent and perceptive work in the field) she reports the ten most frequent comments made to her by men and women in business when she told them what she was writing about. The man invariably scored number one, with a leer—"Must be a fascinating subject!" While number one from women was—"Don't you find it an awfully boring subject?" She comments—"To the girls, the office doesn't seem to be a sexy place at all, just a place."

The truth seems to be that being a secretary only became women's work when men decided that the work couldn't otherwise be done without a new, cheaper, more docile source of labour. Women came into offices as they did into factories, or into nursing, or into the forces, when a crisis, or a change in technology, made their presence inevitable. And immediately all the most fiddling, trivial, repetitive, and lower-paid tasks were handed over to them with many a self-congratulatory sermon about women's rights to equality.

Almost everything men say about secretaries are lies designed to flatter and mollify them. Those who claim, with self-depreciatory candour, that their secretaries could do their job take great care they are never allowed to do so, or rather be known to do so. Office work has been inflated out of all proportion in the last twenty years partly so that man can always have a white-bloused proletariat below him: they are the black immigrants of the clerical world.

And yet men are often secretly envious of the secretary which may account for keeping her busy with domestic-type tasks, and spinning round her such webs of innuendo and speculation. At least, a secretary has an end product, however boring. She has typed so many letters, filed so many copies, filled so many notebooks, numbered so many memos.

What has the great decision maker, the dreamer of possible dreams, the prophet of future trends, the analyser of past successes, got to show at the end of his week? Redundant, when his area of enterprise suddenly shrinks, he often discovers that he is hard put to explain to a new prospective employer exactly what he used to do for his salary.

Just because the secretary is so expendable, so interchangeable, because her skills can be utilised whatever the firm sells, she has reached the first step to freedom. She has freed herself from spinsterhood, from dependence on parents and husbands, from genteel jobs performed at sweated rates at home. The office male's picture of her as a distracting, seductive vision is one way of divorcing her sex from her ability and keeping her from the higher reaches of managements if not from the lower reaches of managers. If some Lysistrata today were to organise secretaries to refuse their bosses' favours in bed, business would go on as usual. But if they were to withdraw all those other peripheral "feminine" courtesies and gratifications, their employers would soon discover themselves out in the cold without a nurse.

"I've come to see you about a friend of mine."

NORA BELOFF in the World of the Political Correspondent

IT was a Saturday evening nearly twenty-five years ago in Brussels, and I was dining with the veteran *Daily Express* globe-trotter, Tom Sefton-Delmer. The news-desk telephoned to say we were leading the paper with a leaked draft of the West European Treaty I had got for them and, after a long talk on how to dramatise it, I returned triumphant to Tom Delmer: "You wait," he said, "when you develop a middle-aged spread they won't bother to coax you along with secret documents and inside information."

The gloomy prediction of an ever-widening girth and an ever-diminishing fund of exclusive stories never materialised. To begin with, owing to the pace of the job, punctuated, in my case, by much panic and calamity, I never got fat. And as long as I preserved my figure I had nothing much else to lose: I had always had a plain face, made particularly unprepossessing (until antihistamine drugs were invented) by a constantly runny nose.

In any case, in our profession, perhaps one should not be too pretty. One of my colleagues at that time, an American girl with a madonna face and saucer-size blue eyes, named Flora Lewis, once got an exclusive interview with Monsieur Jean Monnet, at a time when his European plans were world news. He had asked to see it before it was published and, to everyone's astonishment, refused to release it. It was only much later that I learnt from an aide that he was afraid his preference for this dream-girl might be misinterpreted.

I began life wishing I was a boy, and in journalism there is no doubt women confront special problems. First, the antipathy of many men—more, it should be said, Conservative than Labour—who resent women who can read and write. That is partly made up for by the fact that most men, but especially Tories, feel they have to be gallant to the opposite sex. I was reminded of this with my first story after being appointed the *Observer's* Political Correspondent in 1964. I was investigating whether the Queen (as the *Statesman* had suggested) had anything to do with the choice of Sir Alec as Prime Minister. I found myself in the office of the Conservative Chief Whip, asking a lot of questions about the crucial night. Neither Sir Martin Redmayne nor I were accustomed to this kind of confrontation and, at one point, he told me if I were a man he would have shown me the door.

Then there is the bar on women at clubs, the Oxford and Cambridge Colleges, and El Vino's standing-up bar. Also there are dinner parties given by diplomats or very posh people, where women withdraw after the meal as the conversation warms up. At least, most women do: Miss Jennie Lee refuses on principle to leave.

If the legend were true, and women were really physically weaker and psychologically more retiring than men, we could not begin to compete. In my case I find I can manage with less sleep—and stay sober for more drinks—than most of my colleagues.

As for psychology, I began as a very bashful child, dominated by prettier sisters and cleverer brothers, and needed to screw up enormous courage to say anything at all. But then, as I grew up, I developed a private game of daring myself to say things, so that by my twenties I had so over-compensated for my natural timidity that my temerity made me almost unemployable.

The comfort is that most normal men prefer a woman's company to a man. As for the political women, who are the ones I need to get along with, of whom Barbara Castle is the most famous, they belong with us, in the secret sorority of those who hold their own in a man's world. Mrs. Castle, of course, is well known to use tears to get her way, a technique normally inappropriate for women reporters. I can only once remember, a very long time ago, resorting to it, and then, certainly, not by design.

"The good listener's through there."

"I find it saves enormously on the washing up."

I was Paris correspondent, and to my infinite excitement had just been appointed to Washington. Suddenly, on a foggy day in the middle of a French crisis, I was summoned back urgently. I took the boat-train and was ushered into the Editor's office as soon as I had arrived, to be told that he had received reliable advice that Washington did not take women journalists seriously, so he had better send someone else.

The disappointment was too much. Highly embarrassed to be confronted with a weeping girl, he said, well, maybe he should consult his colleagues? And maybe too I would find it less embarrassing to wait outside? They trooped in, and I stayed in the corridor rehearsing a stiff upper lip and planning to tell them that, anyway, I did not like America. When I was eventually called back in, glasses were being handed round and they toasted my future as Washington correspondent. I took the night-ferry back, having, within twenty-four hours, spent eighteen hours travelling and two-and-a-half minutes in editorial consultation. They were not wasted.

The real trouble is that women are supposed to be more tender than men, and so everybody, from the Prime Minister downwards, applies a double standard to our copy. If one of my lobby colleagues and I reveal something politically disgraceful he will be called "scathing," I will be called "bitchy". If we hurl ourselves after an exclusive story, he will be "dynamic," I will be "pushy". If we ridicule someone, he will be called "humorous," I will be "catty".

It is a hard life, hard-working, hard-hitting, and hard-drinking, but I like it. And looking back I can see that my childhood predilection was misplaced. In journalism it is better to be a woman.

Nora Beloff is Political Correspondent of "The Observer".

"How small do you like your talk?"

Eternally
ffeminine

by ffolkes

*"That's nice of you to say so, Robert, and I appreciate it of course,
but I **do** have a mind too."*

"I must say Mr. Benson, you make chartered accountancy sound very exciting."

*"And **why** are there no women nuclear physicists? Because women believe in Life, **that's** why there are no women nuclear physicists."*

"It's the only way I can get him to eat anything."

"The one in the middle is paying for it."

Should a Lady Ever Doubt Barbara Cartland's Word?

and other problems of etiquette currently besetting GILLIAN REYNOLDS

OH the shame, oh the guilt. Since reading Miss Barbara Cartland's *Book of Etiquette** I can't seem to shake them off. Useless to protest that I didn't have wedding invitations printed on heavy card in silver with bells and bows in the corners, that I never say "lounge" or "Notepaper" or "WC", that there are no musical lavatory paper holders or humorous door plaques indicating that same room, that no china ducks fly across my walls or plants swing from the ceiling. The black marks Miss Cartland awards for such superficialities come nowhere near the ones this book would award me for all round ungracious living.

And I'm honestly sorry for it. To think, if I had read the rules for how to behave when travelling somewhat earlier I might have been having much more fun on public transport, for a start. Miss Cartland's friendly and pleasant manners in railway carriages once brought her, she tells us, a proposal of marriage from a complete stranger with whom she had talked between London and Cardiff. "And," she adds in the next paragraph, "also one from a millionaire who carried my dressing case from a cross-Channel steamer into the train waiting at Dover."

Mind you, even if I had reaped such due rewards for social grace I doubt if the manners of my husband would have measured up to the occasion. At a guess I'd say he'd either accuse me of telling a lie, being drunk, or trying to needle him and I also doubt whether he would have indulged in the spontaneous and genuine outbursts of affection which Miss Cartland says kept the marriage magic. More like he'd have fetched me one to the solar plexus, totally ignoring yet another prime Cartland maxim, "The self discipline of good behaviour should never be dropped within the home, least of all by the husband and wife."

On the home front I fall equally below the standard expected. Miss Cartland sets out her own seven rules for a smooth running happy home, one of which especially takes my eye. "I expect my family to say thank you for an exceptionally delicious meal. When my sons were small they were always sent into the kitchen to thank the cook. They still do this. This is even more important if the mother does the cooking." Now the loophole here is the "exceptionally delicious meal." What if you've never managed one? It's your word and the printing on the baked bean can against theirs

Anon 35p.

after all. I could start the ball rolling in this saying thank you business, I suppose, by bending some of the other Cartland rules to suit my own book.

"Thank you," I could say, "for being on time. For washing and being tidy and for the men wearing a tie and jacket. For clearing up any mess made by your dog or cat and for sending me a letter of thanks for the special festivities of last Christmas." Would this start a new era of harmony, tolerance, consideration and gentleness, I wonder. Would they say, "And thank you, mother, for this exceptionally delicious Spam and chips?"

Love-making has rules too, and saying thank you figures largely in them. "A man who makes love and turns over or goes to sleep without telling a woman how much he loves her and how greatly he has enjoyed himself is both a fool and a brute. But a woman should also thank the man for having made her happy." This all comes after the preliminary required bedroom etiquette of the man opening the windows, the woman setting the clocks and putting out his clean shirt and socks, and remembering too that "It is bad manners for a woman to go to bed with her face covered in cream and equally bad manners for a man who grows hair very quickly to kiss her unless he has shaved." The man must also bear in mind that "Cleanliness is one of the essentials of marriage but it is excruciatingly bad manners to leave the bathroom and the basin in a dirty wet mess for the next occupier."

ffolkes

"*Really? In the Fifteenth Century you could end up here for doing practically nothing.*"

Now that's the sort of thing I could cross stitch onto a fake Victorian sampler and hang on the wall, if only the book didn't tell me such things are lapses from good manners and betray my breeding.

Miss Cartland is really hot stuff on personal cleanliness and hygiene. Washing, shaving, bathing, attention to the due function of the bowels, watching out for dirty hair and body odours are all helped along with cautionary maxims like, "A man pays all his life for the pretty face which has lured him up the aisle," and

"Women were made to give our eyes delight,
A female sloven is an odious sight."

Male readers she asks directly, "How clean are you? Make a list of the times yesterday when you washed your hands. When did you last soap yourself all over?"

This, of course, is in the advice to husbands section. It would never do to flick over the book lightly before going out to dinner at the Duke of Thingy's and thus muddle the rules in this chapter with the later notes on how to converse and hold a knife and fork at a formal dinner. It wouldn't do at all to let such phrases enter the head while turning it alternately between the guest seated on the left and the right and watching where the butler puts his tureen. Still, Miss Cartland does say that when she was bringing up her children she did offer the following advice.

"Talk," I used to say to my daughter. "It doesn't matter what you say, but it's abominably rude to sit eating and saying nothing." So presumably if all else failed one could recall Miss Cartland's observations on history and use them as starters. "The Greeks and Romans, having no soap, relied on loosening dirt by having a slave scrape them with a device called a strigil. They were a clean race."

Actually, there are a good many highly entertaining anecdotes concerning the titled and well bred scattered educationally throughout the slim volume. We hear how the Earl of Caernarvon reduced a dinner guest to tears when she wanted to smoke between courses, though the story itself is told against the smoker. We also hear how a well mannered hostess received the apology from a guest whose visiting footman had dropped a priceless Crown Derby dessert service. "Please don't worry," said the hostess with what Miss Cartland describes as tact, "it was very old."

Obviously, it is my own bad manners and innate lack of breeding which makes me side with the culprits in these tales. I pointed out to my husband that we had seriously erred when in announcing the birth of our children we put in "a brother for . . ." This, says Miss Cartland, is absolutely incorrect, as is the putting of the wife's maiden name or any fancy bits like "the gift of a son". "But," said my husband, "if good manners is not hurting people's feelings and saying thank you all the time, wouldn't we be breaking the rules by

hurting the other children's fraternal sentiments and not blessing Providence?"

This is where Miss Cartland's guide gets a bit like the rules
of *Monopoly*. If you are going by "Family first—in everything!" or "to thine own self be true," you could presumably
skate over such dilemmas with a mere throw of the social
dice. On the other hand, does custom and convention come
first, in which case pay £100 to the Community Good
Manners Chest and miss a turn.

At least I now know how to behave towards Royalty, how
much to tip, how to address living-in-staff,

Housekeeper (almost an extinct race) is called Mrs. by
her employers and the staff whether she is married or not."
how to get ladies out of the room while the gentlemen
drink their port and how long the gentlemen are expected to
remain thus engaged (fifteen minutes), not to let the men in a
holiday party in Germany and Austria sit down to meals with
their coats off and wearing braces, and I am duly warned
against letting a local newspaper talk me into including a
verse, proverb or motto in my eleven year hence silver wedding
announcement.

I also know, from the closing pages of the book, that the
right and wrong way of doing things like these or like using
finger bowls and tipping the cook don't really matter in the
sum total of things. The basic secret of good manners, of the
whole of etiquette, is very simple. And furthermore, if you
read her book carefully Miss Cartland modestly claims you will
not only discover it on almost every page, "It also ensures personal success and every possible advancement." So you see
there is a bit more in this good manners lark than mere
civilised living, basic human respect, and social ease—the
lessons this book can teach you will push you ahead. And what
is this magic formula? "It is to say 'Thank you' and keep on
saying it."

And if you don't yourself consider that to be the genuine
root basis of all social ease and success, at least you have had
the gracious experience of entering the enchanted world of
Miss Cartland where wives say "Thank you" while retaining
their elusiveness and husbands mutter the magic phrase while
delicately asserting their domestic dominance, where children
go out and thank cook, and thank mother for teaching them
the thanking experience, as they write her letters saying thanks
for the school holidays, spent one must presume in the Thank
Tank, thanking twice, or thank without trace.

A Wisbech woman who stepped back three paces and recited
a nursery rhyme, as directed by someone who telephoned her
at her home, contacted the police after deciding it was most
unlikely the exercise had been a GPO test.

(Eastern Daily Press)

Me Tarzan, You Tarzan !

STANLEY REYNOLDS

wonders what happened to Jane

THE air was tangy with the pong of my aftershave so I decided to sacrifice the yummy warmth of the steamy bathroom and finish my *toilette* before the three-sided Edwardian looking-glass in my bedroom: and so there I was, running my matched militaries through my still thick and only occasionally brown rinsed hair, unmanageable as always after a wash and me without a drop of that new set that you simply rub in, leave for three minutes and then simply rinse out—it's nothing short of a miracle the way that new set puts an end to after-washing-hair frizz problems; but she had to go and use it all, although when she last washed her hair is anybody's guess. I suspect, too, she'd been at my body mist—an esoteric French brand that you don't find on men's beauty aid shelves in our shops—given to me by a BEA pilot on the Manchester to Paris route who swears by it; a tiny puff under each armpit in the a.m. and it's goodbye to freshness worries, even, he says, after the tensest of tense moments landing on instruments in a real peasouper or rain and crosswinds or, well, you know what Manchester's like.

I completed the one hundred and fifty strokes with the brace of brushes and was inspecting my gums and thinking about hopping back to the bathroom for a go at the peppermint breath spray but, gosh, I had been up nearly two hours already and here it was Sunday morning and I was looking forward to my morning coffee—black with no sugar—and a slice of dry Melba, and, of course, a shufty at the Sunday papers. I laced a four-foot long, pink and beige Indian hand-blocked scarf round my neck and was just testing whether it fell better on my right or left shoulder when the wife sloped in wearing a pair of house slippers like Barbara Stanwyck wore when she went to the bad in *Stella Dallas* or something and she says:

"I see your friend Germaine Greer is at it again."

"My friend?" I said. "Golly, honey, you're the one who used to write the jokes for her on that Granada Sunday-tea-time-fun-for-granny-and-the-kiddies show. *Good Times* or whatever it was."

"*Nice Time*," she said, "Anyway, it kept you in kaftans didn't it, kiddo?" Mention my wife's career as a gag writer and immediately she turns into some kind of an awful Broadway character out of some Preston Sturges movie or something, I don't know. "Yeah," she said, working her toothpick round to the other side of her mouth, "I remember that kid when she wore knickers. Little Germaine, or, rather big Germaine, a tall gawky kid who came to England from

80

the Outback with nothing but a pair of dancing feet and a Ph.D."

"The trouble with Germaine," I began, but my wife snapped:

"Listen, there's nothing wrong with Germaine Greer that two weeks living up a drain-pipe on the banks of the Ganges wouldn't cure." I puzzled over this remark, then saw it was a reference to the plight of the Pakistani refugees, but the wife was out of my bedroom before I could smile wanly at her joke; she had only come in anyway to borrow my old battledress and combat boots.

I turned to the *Sunday Times* and, sure enough, there was Germaine looking like Chips Rafferty's kid sister or something on the cover of the colour supplement. Inside was a wad of pages from the Woman's Lib ladies, high-powered women all; all eking a modest living hewing books and drawing films out of the stony soil of this man's world: Midge Mackenzie, Jane Arden, Eva Figes—and let me tell you, buster, understains even too embarrassing to talk about wasn't in it. These gals had discovered grit and grime and the secret of the healthy sweat. But, golly, they were going on about it as if that old green moss on the teeth was some kind of new cosmetic or something and like hairy legs had just come over from Christian Dior's or somewhere, which, for all I knew, maybe they had.

On the cover old Germaine had that kind of sun tan you get when you are knocking the American bestseller list apart

"Just cut the cackle, fancy pants, and dye her moustache."

week after week like you were Harold Robbins or Daphne du Maurier or someone; and she was, apparently, living on this little station of hers in Tuscany, with probably like no more than, say, a platoon of peasant help to hang up the spaghetti to dry, stomp on a grape, or bash the odd dirty vest with a rock down by the river; she was sunning in Italy but still fighting the good fight against petticoats, tights, suspender belts, ˙ knickers, girdles, toothbrushes, razors, tweezers, bras, and hot baths. Still, I noticed the dear thing was still plucking the old eyebrows and still able to give out her weight and vital statistics, just like she was Miss Sunny Rhyl 1971 or something, without batting an eye-linered eye in a single moment of hesitation. "Hmmm," I said to myself, "I'll bet she knows her inside leg and all."

Well, I couldn't help from thinking what a topsy-turvy world of great big hairy-chested ladies we are moving into. Next thing you know they'll be raging about like Marlon Brando as Stanley what's-his-name—one of those Polish names with all the letters in the alphabet but the vowels and ending in ski—in *A Street-Car Named Desire* and there's us lily pale men, just like Vivien Leigh, all ghostly despair and a white chiffon scarf, in the Blanche Dubois part. Listen, I'd hate to cast a revival of that play, you'd have to give Marlon the Vivien Leigh role or they just won't believe it any more. It's true; listen, right now I know people who actually read *War and Peace* for the giggle it gives them when that Anatole Kouraguine, you know the Vittorio Gassman one in the movie, seduces the Audrey Hepburn one because it's just so goddamned funny that's why, the whole idea of actually seducing one of them, you know with the waves of influence coming out of your finger tips like in one of those Learn the Power of Hypnotism adverts.

But what I wonder is: what are the future historians and sociologists and those sort of people going to think when they are rummaging about in the dusty old attic of our generation and, listen, they come upon these marvellously preserved old copies of *Playboy, Penthouse, Men Only, Fiesta, Mayfair* and all those mags with the girls looking like those rubber ladies that you blow up that they said sailors used to have and what are they going to think gazing· at Elki and Randi and Sandi and Mandi glowing all tan and pink with nary the blemish, pimple, black-head, nor mole with protruding hair? What sort of mean, dark age of feminine slavery are those flashing white teeth of Carolyn—18, sand-dusted and wet-breasted—Hargreaves-Bland, of *Mayfair* Vol. 6 No. 7, going to speak of to future sociologists?

I mean, all those scanty undies adverts in the classified display pages of the Saturday papers which used to have us schoolboys just groaning· with desire· to grow up fast and face life's harsh realities, they're going to look like some sort of primitive costumes of torture; but what, I'm trying to say, are the schoolboys going to groan about? A hairy calf muscle and a set of receding gums?

I blush for the future my poor boys are going to see, and I tell you, I tore that hand-blocked Indian job from my just too sickeningly white pillar of marble throat, shucked free of my form-fits and searched in vain for my old baggy moleskin trews, just dying to race race race down to breakfast and kick over that carbohydrates, fat, protein, and vitamin-free diet with a fried steak and six eggs.

"What's that look on your mug in aid of then?" she snapped, sitting with her boots on top of the table amidst the clutter of last night's and that morning's dirty dishes, her legs encased in my old baggy moleskins.

"Gee Willikers, honey," I said, "but that table's a mess, mess, mess."

"So," she said, leaping to her booted feet, her lower jaw hanging in simian menace, "you want me to clear the table? I'll clear the table for you," she said, making a motion with her arm just like Brando in *Street-Car* just before he sweeps all the dirty dishes to the floor before the eyes of the horrified Vivien Leigh.

"Now, now, ducks," I cried, "think of the children, think of the neighbours, think of England."

And then, of course, I felt this hand on my shoulder and I awoke and she was standing there with a cup of tea-bag tea, I ask you? and she says, "You can get up now. I've ironed your lavender shirt and the scarf that goes with it."

"Gee whiz, honey," I said, "I've just had the worst dream you won't imagine it."

"And here," she said, "are the Sunday papers. I see your friend Germaine Greer is at it again."

"My friend?" I asked her . . .

"*You never tell me you hate me anymore.*"

Ken Pyne

MODERN SEX WAR ENGLISH USAGE

ANGELA MILNE

Authoress. A word for female author. As used by taxmen *(wife's income as authoress)* it has small annoyance value because in this context it is competing with large annoyance values; but in ordinary life it can be used to imply, however subtly, that the woman author in question belongs to the Romantic Novelists' Circle, and gardens in a raffia hat. *I hear you are quite an authoress/We have with us tonight a gracious and distinguished authoress.* (See also -ESS.)

Clippie, a woman bus conductor, is now obsolete but was coined about forty years ago *(a)* to rhyme with *Nippy,* then the official name for a Lyons waitress, *(b)* to indicate that these new women bus conductors were frilly, eager bundles of goodwill, not to be taken too seriously. It is worth mentioning here because probably its use on the first lot of women bus conductors made the second lot quite happy to be called anything so inoffensive as *conductress.*

-ess. The general rule seems to be that where the use of the female-designating suffix *-ess* is long-established and/or refers to a woman doing a job unquestionably as well as a man, then it does not offend; eg *abbess, actress, seamstress, waitress, stewardess.* The rub comes with terms like *authoress* (see above), and for similar reasons *poetess* and *sculptress. Poetess* is specially offensive because its implications are really rather true. Consider Alice Meynell's *I must not think of thee; and, tired yet strong;* who but a *poetess* could have written those last three words? It is significant (see *authoress*) that Alice Meynell is said to have worn a big droopy hat *indoors.*

-ette is a suffix which diminishes as well as feminises. It was in fashion at a time when feminine invasions of male territory could fairly be considered outrageous, and *suffragette, undergraduette,* were brave attempts to cut female monsters down to size by making them sound like pet midgets. Note how piquantly these epithets contrast with the seriousness of the pursuits they describe. The same cannot be said of *usherette,* which may be why it has survived; or of *drum-majorette,* if it catches on.

Girl Friday. An office factotum when advertised for. The associations with tropical sunshine, scanty informal clothing, inescapable chumminess, lack of routine, the slave trade, etc, are intended to attract applicants, and no doubt succeed.

Girlie, when used as an adjective in conjunction with *girl,* is to some extent (along with *bird, chick, baby* and three hundred and eighty-seven other synonyms) the modern equivalent of -ETTE. *Surprise surprise when a fully-fledged barrister looks like a girlie girl!* (See JOURNALISTIC AMAZEMENT.)

Hurricanes are named after girls "because they are so unpredictable." No comment, except to suggest the female meteorologists would take their work more seriously than to go naming hurricanes after men "because they are so destructive."

Housewife, meaning a married, domesticated woman, is used by men and women alike, with only superficial differentia-

"Perhaps they've decided to go back to my place."

tions of meaning. *Just a housewife,* or *A rotten dreary old housewife,* would for example be spoken by women, while *Clever housewives romp through the day the Fethervac way!* is a typical male statement; but both really mean the same thing. Note that the headline *Housewife wins £45,000* has no masculine equivalent.

Journalistic Amazement, Expressions of. It is common practice for a journalist (be he press, radio or TV), when interviewing a woman who is running, say, a garage or a solicitor's office, to slip back fifty years or more and see her from there. *Isn't it extremely unusual for a woman to take any interest in piston rings (conveyancing)/Don't you as a woman find it extra hard work wrenching nuts with spanners (dealing with difficult men clients)?* are the questions he puts in a desperate effort to make sure his own wife stays home cooking his dinner. If he can add *Now with your blonde hair and smart costume you are if I may say so a very attractive (young) lady*, so much the better. Admittedly some of his interviewees may appreciate this attitude and even trade on it; but to most of the women who read and hear him it remains an effective irritant.

Lady. Now that this word has lost its original meanings (various, from *I know a lady sweet and kind* to *A true lady puts her gloves on before she goes outdoors*), it has become almost exclusively a male weapon in the sex war. *I know all you ladies would like a bit of a gossip together/We find that out pastel fridges have great appeal for the ladies* both hit the mark. But it is perhaps in sporting circles, with *lady drivers, ladies' doubles, ladies' handicap races,* that the word is seen at its best. Note that in the sphere of sport, stronghold of belief in male supremacy, a woman may not keep her maiden name (and the fame that goes with it) but must on marriage start all over again as Mrs. somebody else. This is very ladylike. Note also the subtle difference between *lady drivers,* tolerated participants in a male sphere, and *women drivers,* the people shouted at by men drivers. Most women would settle for being lady drivers.

In general, when men use the word *lady,* they are being their most gallant, i.e. most conscious of their superiority.

"I can't see what you're grumbling about, it's all exactly what they showed in the holiday guide."

Man, Mankind. To pin the word *man* to the whole human race as well as to the male half of it was the best idea men ever had for ensuring their supremacy. It has established the male human animal as the norm, the female as the associate member of the Brotherhood. One cannot talk of the Sisterhood of Man, therefore the human race is, in fact as well as in name, masculine. Poets confuse the issue further: *And, to conclude, I know myself a Man—Which is a proud and yet a wretched thing;* is this (by a male poet) written of Man or of Men? Thus when women read such sentiments they feel they are hovering uneasily on the edge of man's estate, while of course identifying with it. It must be added that any attempt at making things better by dragging woman into generalisations about Man would only make them worse. A dear old professor who got into his lecture a sentence like *Here is one of the qualities which distinguish civilised mankind from primitive people, and civilised womankind too!* would somehow have managed to insult the female sex.

Mini-skirts, Girls in. See *girlie,* and remember that carrying on about girls in mini-skirts (*mini-skirted Carol, 17, in Poodle Rescue*) is as good a way of demoting women as being amazed when they become lawyers or mechanics.

Petticoat. Perhaps women do not mind being told they wield petticoat influence, laughably old-fashioned though the wording may be. But the following *Radio Times* extract: PETTICOAT LINE *This is the programme in which the ladies say what they think about this, that, and the other, without any men around to interrupt with the reminder that "little girls should be seen and not heard"* shows that the word can be associated with an almost obscenely anti-feminist frame of mind and should obviously be kept going.

Prerogative, A Woman's. The first half of a cliché so well known that the second half may be omitted here, as it sometimes is by the man saying it. Its sole interest lies in the fact that it is the only absolutely stock set-form generalisation that men hurl at women.

Secretary Wanted, 19-21. The second half of this, *with good legs,* is always omitted.

World, Miss. In the old days the abstract qualities were often thought of as female persons—e.g. to William Collins the poet, Simplicity appeared as "a decent maid in Attic robe array'd"—and it is perhaps in their place that today's epitomising Miss has arisen; *Miss Garbage Disposal, Miss Blackpool, Miss Frozen Brussels Sprouts* and, of course, *Miss World.* She makes a fitting end to this brief Guide, for, like everything else listed here, she is part of the great male campaign to keep women in their place.

You're a Big Girl Now

ELLEN GREHAN

GYMNAST Jinty's got breasts. The girl's a 36C cup if she's an inch.

Poppy never had breasts. Poppy would Turn Up Trumps, Ride To Win, and occasionally Dance Again. But Poppy wear breasts? Nah, never.

Poppy, I'm going back a good eighteen years now, was a Tokyo Rose of the class war: a composite of all the heroines I remember who used to appear in those weekly girls' comics that were strong on horses, hockey, and midnight feasts in the fourth form dorm. And whose apparent aim was to implant in thousands of eager little working-class hearts an admiration of, and desire for, such middle-class virtues as er . . . well . . . YOU know.

To the children I was brought up among (post-war, Scottish and poor) the strange, all-female, enclosed society of the boarding school as brought to us by courtesy of *Girl's Crystal* and *School Friend* seemed as improbable and exotic as Xanadu. (It took me some time—I was a dim kid—before I grasped the fact that there were girls who were sent away from home to educational institutions even though they hadn't been knocking off gas meters.)

We could scarcely credit a world in which parents only figured as a suggestion of a sensible hat and a well-filled waistcoat come Speech Day. A world in which girls whose names were Monica and Di were forever winning cups and ribbons and God know's what all on the backs of cuddies they called Rajah and Prince. A world in which an apparently

sane child could leap on to a desk and cry: "Remember, girls, the School comes first." And there wasn't a one to throw an inkwell at her.

But ah, lads, times have changed. *Girl's Crystal* has passed away and *School Friend* has merged with the upstart *June*. The half-dozen or so other mags of the ilk that have come into the world since the good old days of The Silent Three—where are they now?—make you realise that you have arthritis where your growing pains used to be. For Poppy and her kind have gone pubescent. They haven't yet got round to giving the Pre-Teen Guide to Orgasm, but the way I see it, give them time.

For where you once had peppy little features on Twelve Ways To Tie A Knot, you now have Personal Freshness for the Under-Tens. Hobby corners that would tell you how to build-your-own-Basilica-out-of-tired-toothpicks now (as in *Diana*) suggest you design a dress. Tasteful snaps of the Royal Family's dogs—aahhh—have given way to pin-ups of pop stars and actors. *Diana* has a gallery of sporting pin-ups chosen by the readers themselves: "Mary Swann of Addington Park thinks Roger Hoy of Crystal Palace is 'the greatest player in the world'". Picture of "the greatest player in the world" showing teeth and frowning.

And who bumped off Brown Owl? She used to come up with ever such handy hints for happy campers. In her place you have an agony column conducted by Angela (of *June and School Friend*) who dishes the dirt thus: "When girls get around to boy friend time, parents naturally become anxious so it's a time to be specially co-operative and show them you're reliable." Too right, Angela.

But, boy friends! Why, in the old *School Friend* ethos a boy was simply a ripping good sort a girl would meet in the

hols, and who was frightfully good at cooking up wizard wheezes to play on his chums. Or some such. The only time they'd touch was when he'd beat her at tennis and thump her on the back with a chirpy: "Hard cheese, old bean."

Take Sally and her Gang in *Girl's Crystal* for instance. There were five of them if I remember aright: three boys, two girls. Aged about 15. Australian. Kind of pre-permissive Barry McKenzies, all big jaws and bonhomie. Now, they were constantly knocking their pan in swimming, and playing croquet, and thumping hell out of each other at all-in wrestling. But never once was there a suggestion that the twang of knicker elastic might be heard in the land.

Another thing. For all their dedication to the Healthy Way of Life, the girls didn't get much out of it apart from huge teeth and a build like a bouncer's. Certainly they did not possess breasts, just a few discreet tucks in their tennis shirts. But Alona the Wild One who currently stars in *Princess Tina* is something else again. When she wears a swimsuit—two piece of course—I swear there's a definite suggestion of nipple.

In the old days, parents were considered an embarrassing irrelevance, like a wart on the nose, and many a heroine thought the clever way to play it was as an orphan with intiguing but safely dead antecedents. But if there were any parents alive offstage then they were always on the side of right. Unless, that is, they were foster or step. The acknowledged Generation Gap has made it possible for stories ("School for Susan" in *Judy*, "Marge in the Middle" in *Mandy,* and "Her Guardian Angel" in *Bunty*) in which it is taken more or less for granted that parents can be a colossal pain in their children's neck. In fact in "Her Guardian Angel" the parents demonstrate their unpleasantness by packing the poor girl off to boarding school . . . as a punishment. Get it?

Yes, boarding schools do still feature to some extent in the adolescent legend. (As do horses. And stories in which the ballerina heroine has broken glass put in her ballet shoes by a rival on the big night.) But generally heroines are not school children as they were in the old days. They're model girls, Lulu type pop singers, nurses, travel couriers, and gym teachers. (Like good old 36C cup Jinty.) And it's changed days since an arch-villain could be defined as someone who'd swipe the Inter-House Sports Cup. Now it's recognised that there is a world outside the bell jar of the school and you have heavies such as corrupt property developers *(Penelope* before it merged recently with *Princess Tina),* sneaky art dealers *(Diana)* and bullying, Rachman-style landlords *(Princess Tina).*

Pupil Power gets featured in *June and School Friend* when the heroine Patsy leads a protest march at her comprehensive because a favourite teacher has been given the boot. No messing about with middle-class old-style remedies such as a massive dose of laxative in the spiteful Head's tea, you'll notice. But straight to the nitty-gritty with the walk-outs, and petitions to the local education chief. That's the spirit.

That's telling them. In another story in *June and School Friend*, dead abrasive stuff, this, there is even—cripes—a suicide attempt. (There's this girl, see, and she crawls out on to a ledge and she's all set to jump. But Sindy—that's Our Heroine—tells her not to. So she doesn't, Whew.) Apart from all the orphans who used to populate the old *School Friend* stories, and who would tell us in the last balloon that they were princesses of one of the more obscure Royal Houses, the only time death ever got a mention, as I recall, was when Dobbin had to be put down after breaking a leg.

Without a doubt the point where you realise that Poppy's world has changed beyond all recognition is when, in *Princess Tina*, a pop group called *Jackie and the Wild Boys* sing "We're young, we're free, it's wonderful to be we."

Such an attitude would have been totally incomprehensible to the Poppy of eighteen years ago, committed as she was to the view that youth was just a place to hang about in while you waited for Real Life to Begin.

Daughter in the House by GRAHAM

"Iain—this boy I met—Iain says that my generation is involved in a struggle to free itself from the morass of apathy in which so many of us are trapped by the dull mediocrity of our middle-class background."

"This is what comes of marrying a career woman." (1950)

Ah, memories ...

Lady (to Committee-room Clerk, who hands her a small bill announcing a forthcoming political meeting). *"But is it possible for ladies to go to these meetings?"*
Clerk. *"Why not?"*
Lady. *"I thought they were more or less of a rough nature."*
Clerk. *"Well, Madam, we've taken every possible precaution to keep out the suffragettes."*

Hostess of Super Picnic. *"This always makes one realise what our poor soldiers went through."*

MOST CONSIDERATE

Mrs. Snobbington. *"We had meant to call long before this, really, but with the best intentions, somehow, we always kept* **putting off the evil day."**

Mamma.	"*Now go and say Good-night to your Governess, like a good little girl, and give her a Kiss.*"
Little Puss.	"*I'll say Good-night, but I won't give her a Kiss.*"
Mamma.	"*That's naughty! Why won't you give her a Kiss?*"
Little Puss.	"*Because she slaps people's faces when they try to Kiss her.*"
Mamma.	"*Now, don't talk nonsense; but do as you're told.*"
Little Puss.	"*Well, Mummy, if you don't believe me—ask Papa!*"

"**There,** *Alice—as if there isn't* **enough** *trouble in the world!*"

THE SUFFRAGETTE THAT KNEW JUI-JITSU
The Arrest.

Albert (gallantly giving way). "Your, Partner!"

THE STRENUOUS YEAR OF

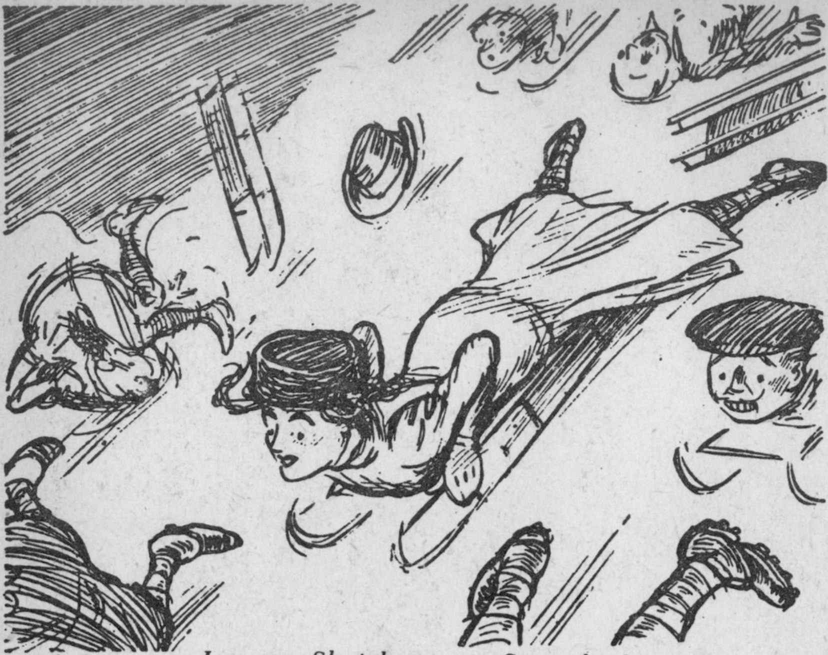

January—She toboggans in Switzerland.

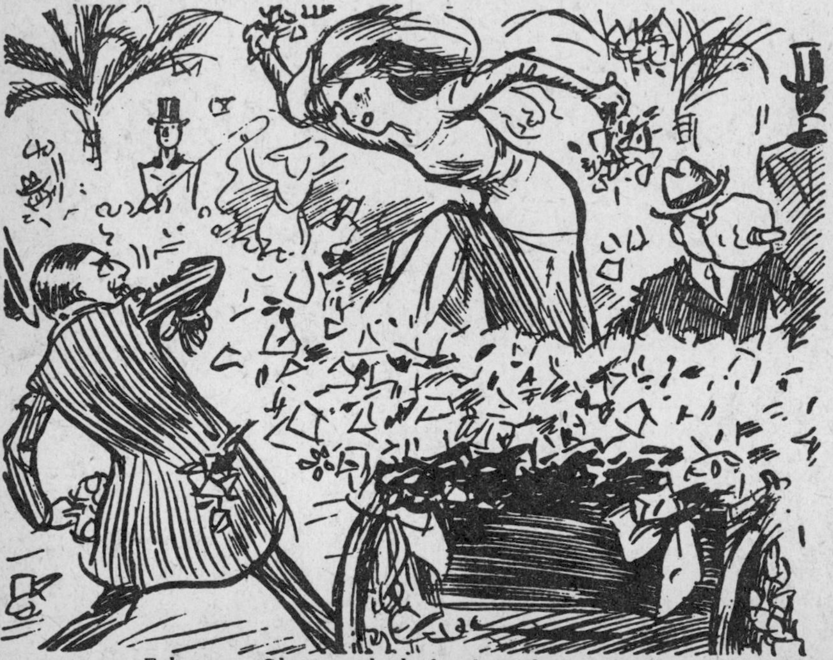

February—She attends the battle of flowers at Nice.

A LADY OF FASHION—1910

March—She breaks the bank at Monte Carlo.

April—She shops in Paris.

THE STRENUOUS YEAR OF

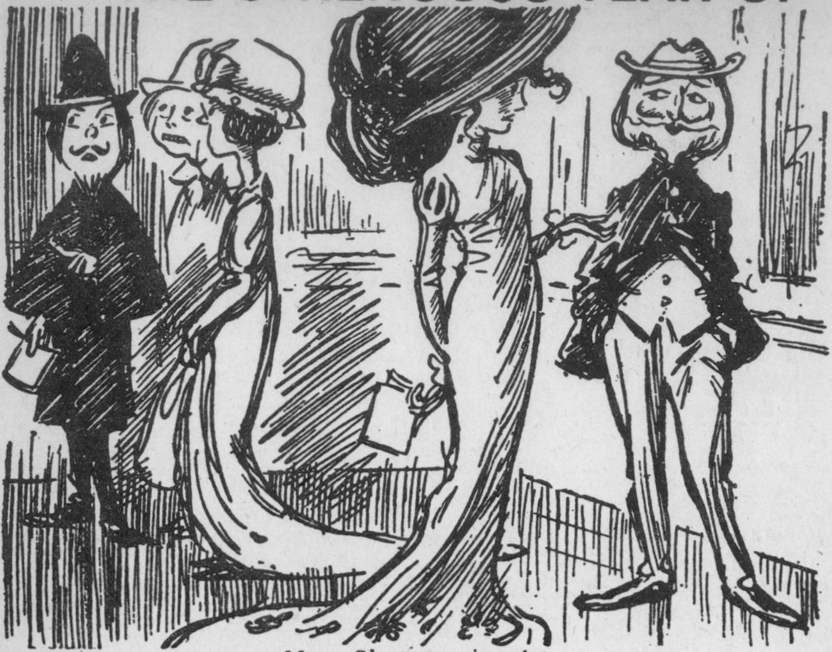

May—She patronises Art.

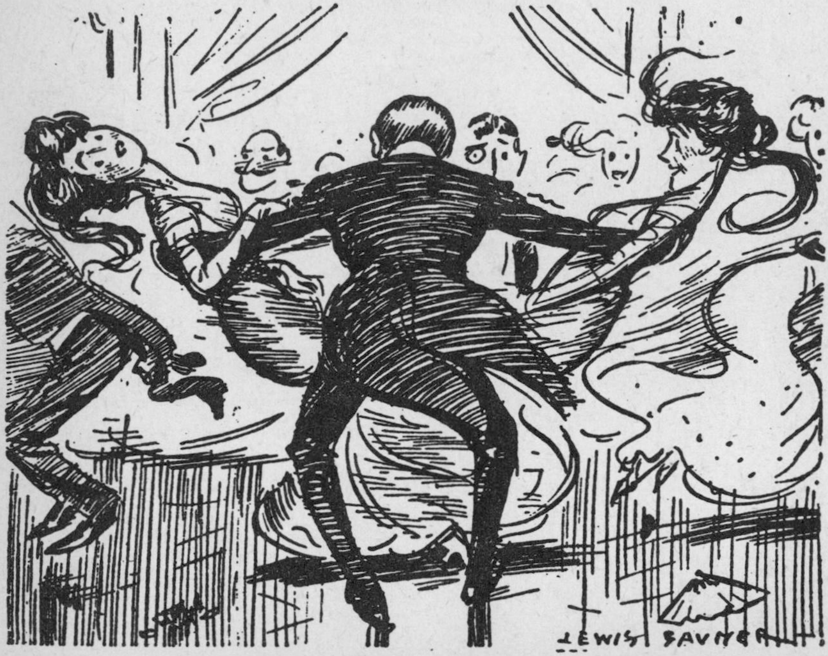

June—She enjoys the whirl of the London Season.

A LADY OF FASHION—1910

July—She attends race meetings.

August—She goes yachting.

THE STRENUOUS YEAR OF

September—She stalks deer.

October—She assists at the shoot de luxe.

A LADY OF FASHION—1910

November—She leads the field with the Quorn.

December—She merrymakes at a smart country-house.

THE FARMER'S IDEA OF THE LANDGIRL

THE LANDGIRL'S IDEA OF THE FARMER

Learning to Swoon Again

DRUSILLA BEYFUS was too young for Thirties style chiffon and champers but eagerly awaits the promised revival. Author, broadcaster, journalist and editor of Brides *magazine.*

THE return of romance is rumoured in the media. As a statement I put it on a par with the news, solemnly spelt out in a newspaper the other day that "sex makes a comeback." Romance is always and forever with us.

Suppose, however, that romantic attitudes become not merely popular, but fashionable, promoted and emulated? One of the many consequences would be a search for a new heroine (a reinstated concept), whose lifestyle, appearance, values and relationships perfectly express the new romantic revival. In films, TV series, novels, magazine serials, she might become as much part of the cultural furniture as, whisper it softly, the groupie girl of the groovy, cool, swinging past.

While everyone is scrabbling around for ideas to help build up her identity, I have thoughtfully produced a few clues. The Credo for a girl who goes romantic might be as follows:

I believe in being chaste and chased, and will not apologise for reviving such a corny old pun, as much of my new lifestyle depends on a confident reworking of tried and trusted old themes.

I promise to donate every pair of tights, my see-through blouse and my unisex bathing trunks to the tombola at the forthcoming Danny La Rue Benefit. At all times I shall sit with my legs crossed and not fling them about any old how as if it did not matter. I will do my best to ensure that when such lapses occur it will matter to men. As a founder member of the campaign to help stamp out boring erogenous zones, I am prohibited from giving a graphic description of the chiffon, silken and elasticised mysteries which enshrine my person in place of neuterising tights.

I shall be content to receive one perfect rose, or one perfect jonquil will do, providing that my suitor swears he has kissed it first. This will take my mind off Dorothy Parker's speculation that one perfect rose is just my luck, why not one perfect Cadillac?

Men hoping to win my favours who adopt a casual recreational approach to sex will be dimissed as old fashioned and hung-up on permissiveness. If this does not do the trick I shall cry. Tears, large, lustrous, welling, will never be very far away these days, and when nature fails I will rely on my tortoise-shell and silver tear dispenser. I carry this around with a companion piece, a container of sal volatile for shocks, such as rediscovering that men are beasts and only want One Thing. There is plenty of room in my reticule (in petit-point embroidery) recently emptied of its load of pot, pills and cigars.

I swear to reform my taste in posters on the wall at home. Down will come Che Guevara, Flower Power, psychedelic-pop and Hells Angels and up will go portraits of the giants of modern romance, Tolstoy, Flaubert, Stendhal, the Brontë's for the oldies, and coming up to date with Barbara Cartland, Denise Robins and Erich Segal of Love Story. My collectors pieces will include blow-ups of Dr. George Steiner and John Sparrow, Warden of All Souls, for his poetic defence of passionate love in *The Times* recently.

I need rescuing, but my lovers must possess a background with classically romantic associations. I shall continue to cast myself as a maid of humble station (no change here as this one paid off in the bad old swinging days), and will succumb to men whose infatuation for me will rise above such petty ties as class, and family and country. We shall, in Byron's words, be "all in all to each other." But not before a great deal has gone on before. It will be love at first sight. Time will stand still. Somewhere along the line we shall vote the world well lost for love. I may thwart him a little to keep him up to the mark. Life will be sad as romance is always sad. Even when it is happy.

As from now I will be turned on by moonlight, nightingales, the picturesque architectural ruins of antiquity in far-away climes, desert islands, sunsets, waves beating against a seashore, "I'll Be With You In Apple Blossom Time" played softly on the ivories. I shall lose my cool forever.

I am pinning my all on a look first popularised in the Victorian sentimental painting "April Love" by Arthur Hughes. Rosebud lips, a flitting blush and a modest stance have taken over from take-me-or-leave-me boldness. My face will be heart-shaped, registering all the notes from submissiveness to compliance, in mulish defiance of Women's Lib.

My make-up has changed. I have consigned my tear-proof, cling-proof, kiss-proof cosmetics in the Come Looking Great range made by Orgasma to the attic (where one day my

"I suppose you meant well, Daddy, but you never gave me things I really needed, like poverty."

grandchildren will excitedly discover them beneath mildewing dustsheets), and gone over to the Born to Blush products. I am to look vulnerable, easily bruised, delicate.

Also I am through with all that old-hat honesty about telling the truth when asked if one's beauty is real or out of a box. Long live the new social hypocrisy which permits the use of the protective little white lie. My fringed eyelashes and wayward curls are real, sir. And that should put a stop to the practice in pre-romantic times of his asking to borrow them both.

Will she really happen, this absurd romantic creature? Before dismissing her presence even in fictional form as wildly improbable, consider the lunatic lengths to which the counter movement, social realism, has gone. Only yesterday I heard the NASA authorities refer to the wives of the moon shot men as "primary contacts." We may need a shot of April Love.

"I forgot the salt."

Young Man. "But surely you know me. I rescued you from drowning only yesterday."

Girl.   "Really! How nice of you! Morning or afternoon?"

Counterweight

ALAN COREN

"I'm quite sure within the next two decades we shall have all the
girls at Woolworth's with degrees."   *Edward Short, MP*

"NOTHING much. Went up the Royal Festival same as
usual with Norman."

"That's the skinny biochemist from Smokers Sundries,
innit?"

"Yes. I wore me spotted winceyette with the velveteen bow."

"Nice. Anything good on?"

"Only bloody Arnold Schonberg, that's all?"

"You must be joking, Doreen! Not *Verklärte Nächt* again?"

"Only bloody *Verklärte Nächt* again, that's all!"

"I wouldn't care, it's not even dodecaphonic."

"That's what I said to Norman. It's not even bloody
dodecaphonic, I said. It's *early* Schönberg. That's not what I
call value for money, I said."

"You might as well be listening to Stravinsky, Doreen."

"You might as well be listening to bloody Stravinsky.
That's what I said to him. If I'd known, I wouldn't have gone
home and changed. A short skirt's good enough for early
bloody Schönberg."

"What did he say, Doreen?"

"He said it was seminal. He's so bleeding crude sometimes."

"I don't know why you go out with him. He only went to
Trinity College Dublin and his breath smells. It's not as if
you weren't a brain surgeon."

"To tell you the truth, Vera, I—would you mind keeping
your little boy's fingers off them chocolate peanuts, madame,
thank you very much!—to tell you the truth, I'm thinking of
giving Norman the bullet. I met this very nice bloke at the
Selfridge's Electrical Appliances Department party last
Friday—"

"I was going to that, only the cat got into me wigbox
Thursday night and did sunnink. How was it?"

"Very nice. It was to commemorate the anniversary of
Spinoza's first marriage. They had them little bridge-rolls with
roe in them."

"I've always liked Spinoza. You know where you are with
the *Tractatus Theologico-Politicus*. He's never flash, is he? If
there's one thing I can't stand, it's a flashy determinist."

"I know what you mean. That's exactly what I said to this
fella I was telling you about. He works in Plugs & Flex. You
wouldn't think so to look at his hands: they're all big, including the fingers. You wouldn't think he'd have the nimble-
ness for flex."

110

"We're going in for reading."

"I've always liked big hands. You know where you are with big hands. What's his speciality?"

"Ooh, you are awful sometimes, Doreen!"

"I didn't mean that, you silly cow! I mean, where was he before Plugs & Flex?"

"Balliol. First in Mods, First in Greats. They say he knows more about Kant than anyone on the first floor."

"Doreen!"

"Immanuel."

"There's people looking, Dor. Anyway—"

"Anyway, turns out this fella's got two tickets for the first night of the Bucharest Citizens' Marionette Theatre production of *Aida*, and would I come?"

"You don't half fall on your feet, Doreen."

"I know. It was bloody smashing, Vera! I'd never heard a baritone puppet before. And you know that bit where Rhadames returns in triumph with Amonasro—"

"—the Ethiopian king—"

"—the Ethiopian king, right, well instead of elephants, they had ferrets with little rubber trunks on. And all these little puppets were singing in Rumanian!"

"Fantastic! What did you do after?"

"Went up Spitalfields, din't we? Had another look at the Christchurch lintels."

"You can't never have enough of Hawksmoor, that's what I always say."

"Well, yes and no. Personally, I never went for the north quadrangle of All Souls."

"I never went for All Souls at all. That bloke who demonstrates artificial lawn's a Fellow of All Soul's. He's got a hairpiece. He's a bit funny, if you ask me. There was just the two of us down the stockroom last Wednesday, he come up to me and his face was all shiny, and he was trembling, and I thought: Hello, Vera, good job you got your body stocking on, and do you know what he wanted?"

"What?"

"He said could he hold my shoes for a bit."

"Go on!"

"Honest."

"What did you say?"

"I said, I'll let you hold one of them, Doctor Strude-Pargiter, but I don't think we ought to go all the way on our first date!"

"Oooh, Vera, you're worse than I am! What did he say?"

"He said he'd written the definitive footnote on the Edict of Worms and he thought that entitled him to certain privileges. So I told him about how my mum would never let me go out with a mediaeval historian, and us ophthalmologists are only happy with our own kind, and I think he understood. I didn't want to hurt his feelings, and I could see that gum running down his forehead with the excitement and everything, so I come upstairs again."

"Very wise. Is it lunchtime yet?"

"Not for another eight minutes and forty-one seconds. Why?"

"I want to go up the travel agent's, don't I? Leave it too late, everywhere's booked up."

"Going anywhere nice?"

"I thought I might try the ten-day cruise of the fjords, only forty-nine guineas, including headphone. You visit sites of the Old Norse Sagas, and in the afternoons well-known philologists discuss famous textual cruces on deck, if wet in the first-class dining-room. There's semantics every evening, and a gala ball on the Saturday when everyone comes as the troll of his choice and gets rotten drunk. Alice Prior in Plastic Binettes nearly got pregnant twice last year, and she's only ever read *Beowulf* in Penguin, so it just shows you. Tell you what, Vera, whyn't you come with me? It wouldn't half be a giggle, or *gögl*, as the Eddas put it."

"It's ever so nice of you to suggest it, Doreen, but I don't think it's me, really. I think I'll just stay in the library again this year, there's no swimming, of course, but it's warm, and there's always a few people from the British Home Stores boning up on something or other, they're ever such a friendly crowd."

"Vera Collinson, you can't pull no wool over *my* eyes! I know what you're up to, you sneaky bitch, you're working on that thesis of yours, right? *Zygostereopy In The Retina Of The Potto, Clinical Observations Towards A Classification, by Miss Vera Collinson?*"

"Oh, Doreen, I din't want to tell no one, not even you! It's just—you won't take offence?—it's just that I want to, you know, better myself. I want to get on. I don't want to sell Smarties in Woolworth's forever! And if I had a Ph.D., Doreen, I could leave all this behind me, I could make something of myself, I could *be* someone, I could get somewhere!"

"My Gawd, Vera, you're not thinking of . . ."

"Yes, Doreen, Marks & Spencers!"

"You're a mad ambitious little fool, Vera Collinson! But—but I admire you!"

"Don't cry, Doreen, love. There's other things in life, you'll get married, have kids, you see if you don't, it'll all—"

"If only I had the application for original research, if only I had the academic stamina, if only I'd kept up—yes, madame, a quarter of hazelnut cluster, madame, right away, madame, no thank you, madame, quite all right, I just got something in my eye, that's all, madame, that'll be seven pee, thank you very—sob—much."

"Look, Mary, I must go; I started leaving my husband an hour ago."

The Best Jobs Get The Best Clothes

PRUDENCE GLYNN explains how

THOUGH not one to leap forward readily with ammunition for Women's Lib., professional interest prods me to point out that fashion for men and women offers a fine example of inequality of opportunity. Threshing about in the cul-de-sac of bra-burning and knicker-discarding as they are, the liberationists seem to have missed the point that being able to wear what you like when you like is not remotely as satisfactory as having a chance to wear something spectacular, for real and not for fancy dress. Maybe the best jobs go to men; the best dressed jobs certainly do.

I arrived at this belief not via emotion but via observation for when I began to write about men's as well as women's clothes I soon realised, after reporting actual events, that the former were much more interesting than the latter. Take the most obvious example, horse racing. While you shiver in your floating chiffon panels and tittup through the aftermath of a sudden summer shower, some skinny jockey is going to flash up wearing the most sensational combination of colours cut in the only shape that looks right in all weathers and he wears light boots, too. Motor racing is worse; the 24-hour race at Le Mans was peppered with beautiful girls looking soignée in Courrèges battle-dress tops and little quelques choses by St. Laurent but then out came the drivers wearing all those badges and signs and flashes, dressed in gold cloth from shoulder to ankle and topped off with helmets as dramatic and romantic as anything out of Sir Walter Scott.

Which brings me to the fighting services. Women of course wear uniform in the services too, but they hardly look romantic; more often they look apologetic, because it's Bowdlerised gear and was probably designed originally with some savage and frisson-inspiring purpose deemed quite unsuitable, by the guardians of the morals of the women of England, to be worn by Our Brave Girls. And anyway women never seem to be at the right rank or in the right post to wear the real dazzle. Launch a ship and at your elbow will be some alluring naval figure dressed to look calm, impressive, important, with lovely medals and that subtle flash of gold. He will look absolutely right; you will be flapping about your handbag and wondering whether it is considered unlucky to wear green. General MacArthur was my hero for years entirely on account of his hat, which had more gold braid on it than a cinema doorman's, and those dark glasses. I thought him much more sexy than any drab civilian like Cary Grant. Even men's evening dress, about which they are always moaning, is more dramatic than anything women can wear. Black and white is surely the choicest of all colour combinations, the perfect foil for orders and medals and jewels and ribbons and things. Certainly women can get to mayor, but the chain looks better on a man—none of those little gold pins at the neckline. Think of the appeal of cowboy clothes—just clothes men actually work in; think of the matador's Suit of Lights, a fairy story costume with a built-in raison d'être.

But the greatest inequalities of opportunity show up at any traditional English function involving the Monarchy. I once covered the Opening of Parliament and I must say that the ladies got very few lines of print. I really only paused to decide who had the biggest tiara before I was wallowing in the robes of the gentlemen. What a transformation; normally moth-eaten and suspect figures were concealed in sweeping scarlet; oh, the uniforms and gold braid and the swords and the little black patent leather boots. If women wear knee-breeches and black silk stockings they look like Little Lord Fauntleroy, but the Lord Chancellor looks majestic—because he is not wearing his costume for whim but because it goes

"There's an element of mystery about them. They dress abominably, and yet they haven't even got money."

with his job. How extraordinarily pursuivable the extra-ordinaries and pursuivants or whoever they are looked, even though I do remember thinking that contact lenses should be de rigueur with such lavish outfits. The only woman whose job carries equal clothing rights on these occasions is the Queen, who has the routine beautifully at her fingertips, but I cannot see that post is likely to become vacant.

Have you noticed that it is the best dressed religious denominations which are least keen to let women into their executive ranks? I can go without those little skull-caps, but the Cardinal's hat has definite panache and what about those piquant little black four-cornered styles with a pom-pom on top? Purple and scarlet are so flattering, what about those elegant gaiters, what about those crow-black soutanes with all the little covered buttons that the clergy sweep about Rome in? Even the Church of England has fashion sense. I once went to a function attended by the Archbishop of Canterbury only to find that our *tenue de gala* was very nearly the same colour but not quite. I clashed with the Primate (sartorially you understand) and felt it necessary to keep one of our neutral toned spouses between us all evening. What was so irritating was that my dress was the result of hours of indecision and labour and his was part of the post. Observe the bishops in the House of Lords and see what an advantage they have in debate. What Christian patience may be implied by a folding of the lawn wings, what indignation with the puffing of the sleeves. Even the smartest peeresses don't get a look in.

So it is not surprising that men with no official outlet for fancy dress put on such bizarre clothese in their leisure hours and I suppose it is not surprising that women have taken to aping men's legitimate fashions. We've had the army badge craze, the old carpenters' dungarees craze, and now—heaven preserve us—it is suggested that you buy old army boots and spray them with gold paint. It is pathetic, as much a red herring as bra burning. By all means let us wear weird and wonderful clothes but I am enough of a purist to think that good design is always appropriate design. The logical fashion step for liberated women is to demand a high powered dress to go with the high powered job.

While taking driving lessons, I fell for my instructor. He took advantage of this and frequently stopped for kissing sessions. As a result, I failed my test. I need more lessons but I've gone right off him. What do I do?   *(Woman's Own)*

McNicoll said in court: "She knocked me over with the pram and then hit me on the head with a No-Waiting sign—a plastic one. This is what happens every time I see her."
          (Edinburgh Evening News)

116

Miles Kington's Guide to Rich Women

GUIDE-BOOKS

There is a very good reference work on the fathers of rich women called *Who's Who*. It gives details of their addresses and hobbies and books they have written and people they used to be married to, and as rich women always think a lot about their fathers you will have a great deal to chat about.

SHARES

Very few rich women are actually quoted on the market. This is because they never say anything interesting. Emma de Rothschild once said: "The only cure for poverty is bankruptcy," but nobody heard her say it.

HUSBANDS

Most rich women are married to rich men. You can't blame them. Wouldn't it be awful to be married to someone *you* had to give pocket money to? Moral: if you are poor, don't marry a rich woman. Seduce her. Everyone will feel better.

DIET

Rich women often feel pangs of guilt at spending so much money on food, not to mention getting a little too fat. They then read diet systems in *Vogue, Harpers-Queen, The Times* and other faddish papers, all recommending them to subsist on grapefruit and yoghurt for a sennight. So they start buying grapefruit and yoghurt. So what? So, start hanging around grapefruit and yoghurt shops, you schmuck. You cretin, if you're gentile.

CRETIN

Did you know that cretin comes from a Swedish word for Christian? Apparently it referred to one of the more lunatic sects of Protestant. Rich women love this sort of extraneous information.

CABARET

Rich women are almost always bored. What they need is entertainment. Nothing easier than to form a small act, advertised thuswise: "Rich. women a speciality for *The Three Gigolos*. Hire us for your *intime* parties—members of the audience married on request."

MORE PHILOLOGY

Did you know that schmuck is one of 27 Yiddish words all meaning "the sort of man who won't marry the girl his mother tells him to marry"? Why not ask your mother if she knows any rich women you can sponge off? Explain to her that she will always come first with you, and you will be back each night by 10.30.

"No kidding? You mean I haven't just proposed to a poor but beautiful young student struggling through college?"

"It's 'Which?' magazine, sir. One of their tests . . ."

JOB ANALYSIS

Statistics show that rich women are confined to surprisingly few professions. There are no rich office cleaners or teachers, for instance. There are some rich female actresses and writers, but most millionairesses are simply housewives, if you can call having a couple live in to start your labour-saving devices for you being a housewife. Emma de Rothschild describes herself as unemployed but busy.

WHERE?

Where what?

WHERE ARE ALL THE RICH WOMEN?

Rich women tend to flock together on small islands or yachts, where they hang about on street corners or fo'c'sles looking rather pitiful. Just go up to them and tell a joke or ask them to go to the cinema. It's little ordinary touches like this they so desperately miss in their lives. If anything should come of it, don't be offended if they tip you. And try to mention this column.

CONVERSATION

Rich women hate it when you talk about their money, as they assume that that's what you are in it for. Curiously though, they don't mind you talking about the things that money can buy, partly because this is the only thing they can talk about. Nobody ever said accusingly of a gigolo, "He only loves me for my box at the opera."

CORRESPONDENCE

The correct way to start a letter is "Dear Rich Woman" and it should be signed "Yours Fawningly"—never "Yours Faithfully," as this smacks of insincerity. The envelope should be marked Strictly Personal.

BOX AT THE OPERA

Box at the opera? Why not? Nothing could be more refreshing than a quick sparring contest with the rich woman of your choice to the sounds of *The Magic Flute*. Emma de Rothschild once went three rounds with an ex-pupil of this column on a Wagner evening and said afterwards, "I'll go into *The Ring* with any man in the house."

FASHION NOTES

Some rich women dress well, but most just dress expensively. Hide in the changing room of any top class couturier, emerge from behind the curtain when the first rich woman comes in and say "Thank God I've bumped into somebody interesting at this dreadful party." Then zip her up and you're away.

THE HONEYMOON

The honeymoon is perhaps the best part of being with a rich woman, especially if you get rid of the husband for a while. Pretend to be a ski instructor on holiday. Pay for the first drink if you must, but all the rest of the spending must come from her. Send flowers up to her room the whole time. There will be lots around the hotel in pots and vases.

COLOUR

Under the effect of too much money, most women go a peculiar shade of brown all over. Don't comment on this, as they think it is a natural process.

"I'd say divorce the pig this instant, but then I'm only a wrong number."

"Can't understand all this talk of abolishing Public Schools . . .

. . . When I think of mine, with the Inter-House cricket matches . . .

. . . the comradeship of the dorm . . .

. . . cold showers on wintry mornings or fagging for one's Pre . . .

. . I can't help feeling an education like that . . .

. . . does something for a girl."

A Lady is helping the Police with their enquiries

With Winifred Taylor, the first woman detective at Scotland Yard, the field is now wide open. At least, for Bill Tidy.

"Blimey, Super, info on the Midland Bank job's worth more than rissoles and chips!"

"Come out Ridley—no thanks—you haven't got a chance!"

"No thank you, madam. Not while I'm on duty."

"I hate rotten stinkin' lousy coppers!"

"Sergeant Briscoe wants a little chat with you, Fierelli."

"Oh dear, Claudio's having an awful time deciding where to fit the truncheon."

Out of Strong Came Forth Sweetness

ALAN BRIEN walks in beauty

BEAUTY is only skin deep—but then how deep would you expect it to be? No woman was ever actually improved by being flayed. Inner beauty, a quality much praised by head teachers, advice columnists, followers of the cult of St. Mug, fathers of large families, is probably best left to be probed by surgeons and gynaecologists. As commonly used, it simply means—"ugly but resigned to it".

Outer beauty is what painters, photographers, gossip writers and publicists, and Dr. Roy Strong's current exhibition at the National Portrait Gallery, are on about. Beauty is said to be in the eye of the beholder which is usually taken to mean that there is no objective, universal standard. Every one of us can find somebody who thinks we are beautiful if only we can track down an observer myopic enough. And it is true that circumstances alter faces.

When five girls share a flat, one of them is the recognised beauty. The sole female on a two-year Arctic expedition no doubt, after a few months, gets to feel and even look like Helen of Troy. But in a mixed, populous community, so the sociological surveys seem to prove, there is a general agreement about the definition of beauty. And what is more surprising, and slightly depressing, is that males and females seem to seek out the partner who holds the same rank in the hierarchy of pulchritude. To-those-that-have-shall-be-given is a rule which operates with beauty as with money—and everyone else always seems to have more of it than you do.

I have always been rather sorry for beautiful women—and not just because beauty is a flower which wrinkles will devour. Queens have died both young and fair, but at least that's better than being a scullery maid who dies both young and plain. Beauty decays with age, as does every other human attribute. What is pitiable about a beauty is not only that this is usually all she's got, she often finds it difficult to believe that she has actually got it. No one is beautiful marooned alone on a desert island, and I suspect the same doubts plague the beauty alone in front of the bathroom mirror.

You only have to watch the beauty at a party to see the drawbacks. She clears a pathway through the close-packed uglies as if wearing an invisible crinoline, and when she stops a force-field builds up around her like a cage round a parrot. Either she stands alone, being eyed by the other women and avoided by the men, or she attracts that ghastly breed of male, the beauty-kidder. There is something about the beauty which brings out the hair-puller in the opposite sex—the desire to ruffle, disturb and even to punish her for not resembling their wives and girl-friends. They want to take her, and not just her dress, down a few pegs. *Il faut souffrir pour être belle.* And they will show her *comme il faut.*

To be a beauty is almost by definition to be a bore, or even worse, to be expected to be a bore. Like all celebrities who are celebrated for attributes over which they have no control and can claim no merit for possessing, beauties have the power of inhibiting small talk. With the Queen of the Ball, as with the Queen of the Realm, what can you say that has not been said before? I had a mate once who thought he had invented the most intriguing opener for such conversations. He would ask—"Do you speak to imperfect strangers?" But the liveliest reply he ever got was "I think there must be some mistake."

Ordinary women may not be able to stop a taxi by the crook of a little finger, but they do get treated by unknowns as people to be approached, rather than works of art to be evaluated. Standards of beauty may be uniform at any one time in any one society, but they have varied through the ages and in different countries. In an ideal world, I suppose, all fat girls could emigrate to Turkey, and girls with pendulous lower lips large enough to accommodate a fair-sized bangle would be adopted by the Ubangi. Or else, plastic surgery could be on the National Health. But so long as beauty is a rarity, its possessors are likely to find themselves acquired for display rather than use, exhibited as status symbols. And living by the face, die by the face, or be relegated to the back of the shelf when they start showing too many cracks in the facade.

The Masque of Beauty exhibition sets out to show the consistencies and inconsistencies in our view of beauty over the last four hundred years. Dr. Strong claims to have discovered an alternation between the classic and the romantic styles. Classic is angular, hard outlined, statuesque, depending

on the chiselling of the silhouette, the continuity and precision of the modelling: the Tudors, the Augustans, Regency, High Victorians, the Twenties and the Sixties. Romantic is less demanding, swallowing, even embodying, defects, soft, transparent, fluttering, mobile and composed of curves: the Carolines, the early Victorians, the Edwardians, the Thirties and now the Seventies.

Personally, I would say this was the difference between being beautiful and being attractive. The beauty, in my beholding, is always finished, complete, already poised on the verge of being past her best, needing nothing and no one, not even that most fashionable of matching accessories, a man. Perhaps that is why so many men of power struggle to own one, and having succeeded cannot think what else to do with her, except keep her in a strong box at the bank. The romantic women are always on the move, always transient, about to change their clothes or re-disorder their hair, accessible but unbuyable, willing to offer the end of the lease but never the freehold, free but not cheap, open to the winds, tangible yet elusive, and not afraid to show fingerprints.

Beauty is aristocratic, traditional, dependent on courtiers, servants, hangers-on, transported with sign reading "Fragile—This Side Up". Attractiveness is democratic, individual, self-propelling, at home jostling with crowds, appealing to all sexes and classes. If it has any sign, it is "Perishable—Use No Hooks". Beauty is snob appeal, attractiveness mob appeal.

The Masque of Beauty is a scratch, ad-hoc show, giving the impression of being hustled together to meet the deadlines of a colour supplement. The past is represented by paintings from the cellar, the present by photographs from the files. They are set in a spot-lit, windowless maze furnished with shrubbery which is either dead or plastic. The same could be said of the exhibits.

As a piece of light-hearted scholarship even, it scarcely bears out Dr. Strong's thesis about classic and romantic beauty. A lot of the classic beauties are far from "perfection of feature and form". Many of them look like sisters, sometimes brothers, with long, fleshy noses and lips like doorsteps, young bucks worrying about running to fat. It is understandable that the beauties of earlier centuries should nearly all be noble, by birth or marriage. Few milk-maids or fish-wives could afford to slip out and have a snapshot taken by an artist. But to include Queen Elizabeth I, the very epitome of a virgin Queen between those pinched, purse-string lips it would be difficult to insert a hairpin let alone the fine edge of a tongue, is to slavishly pay homage to the hierarchical heresy that the most powerful must always be most beautiful. No doubt it was necessary to pretend to believe this at the Elizabethan Court, but Dr. Strong is hardly likely to have his head chopped off today for rejecting her.

And is it necessary to insist that the modern examples

should include so many titled women (eleven out of thirty-five)—many of whom are scarcely household names, even in households which take the *Daily Express* whose William Hickey column will seemingly include anybody who is kinsman to a second baronet?

If you yearn to know why beauty is sometimes a term of abuse, and will enjoy the malicious pleasure of seeing some talented artists (such as Cecil Beaton and Augustus John) at their feeblest, then the Masque of Beauty will be an enjoyable outing. The most attractive women there are usually courtesans or upper-class rebels, or women's libbers before their time. None of them is a beauty. The most exciting (beauties are not exciting, usually potently anaphrodisiac) is Nell Gwynn in the Lely portrait, naked, languorous, exhausted but probably still game, the sort of picture Charles II would keep to show off to his friends. But she is clearly her own mistress as well as his—and her attractions are as powerful today as then. This is supposed to be the permissive age—are all our modern "beauties" only heads out of *Debrett*?

"This one for you is marked 'Strictly Personal' but it isn't really."

Bacchus Is a Lady

HELEN LAWRENSON

THERE are exceptions, but when most women get sloshed, the gamut of their antics is circumscribed. They may get the giggles, talk too loudly or too honestly, flirt with the wrong men. At worst, they either pass out or throw up. Men not only indulge in these last two practices, sometimes simultaneously, but they also display a variety of other objectionable traits. They want to fight waiters, barmen, doormen, taxi drivers, their best friends, strangers on the street. If thwarted, they want to fight you. They break things. They lose their hats, scarves, coats, glasses and even, on occasion, their teeth. They lose their money too and they give away £5 notes as tips under the impression they are handing out a quid at a time.

Women simply don't behave in this way. Very few women, for example, go out and get rolled. They may lose an earring once in a while but it is usually in the process of trying to ward off a drunken male. Women seldom challenge anyone to a bout of fisticuffs, and they don't throw their money around trying to act like Goodtime Charlies. Nor, as a rule, will you find a group of grown women standing at a bar singing nostalgic songs.

Then there is the business of liquor and sex. The more a man drinks the firmer becomes his conviction that physically he is irresistible. He frequently seems to be working on the theory that possession is nine-tenths of the battle and that if only he can get a good grip on you, especially in the back of a taxicab, you are his. Once safely on bed or couch, the problem is certainly not solved. Drinking does not improve a man's amorous technique. While it is true that alcohol may act as an aphrodisiac, too much of it will make your ithy-phallic paramour's passion more vocal than focal. As ancient Chinese proverb might have had it: leer on face, no lead in pencil.

Another extraordinary thing that happens to men when

129

drinking is that they lose their powers of articulation. They mutter and mumble and whistle their "s's" and repeat every third word for emphasis like the straight man in a music hall comedy skit. They like you to listen with rapt enthusiasm even though no Rosetta Stone has been discovered to translate their unique babble into something resembling a known tongue. I have seen this process of disintegration under alcohol take place with MPs and merchant seamen, authors and editors, ambassadors and actors, tycoons, insurance salesmen, dockers, solicitors and even an anthropologist or two.

Why, in my lifetime I have seen more Solons turn into boozey slobs than I could shake a swizzle-stick at, but rarely have I seen a plastered Portia lose her cool. I was once asked to leave a Havana restaurant called Los Industriales with my escort, an American Brigadier-General, because he suddenly decided, when in his cups, to relieve himself in a corner of the dining-room. (This is a fairly common manifestation among male inebriates. A notorious incident also took place in Havana involving either a famous actor or the equally well-known son of a world statesman—I've forgotten which for the moment—who used the statue of José Martí as a public urinal. It became a minor international crisis in commemoration of which I wrote a couplet: Never pee/On José Martí.)

All that a man has to do when he goes drinking is to drink. A woman, however, has to match him glass for glass because it annoys a man's man if his man's woman doesn't keep up with him. In addition, she must act as nurse, bodyguard, valet, secretary, cashier and interpreter. She must divert him tactfully from quarrels, quiet him when he bursts into song, watch over his money, remind him to get his briefcase from the cloakroom. If he is sick, she must comfort him. If he passes out, she has to see he gets home all right. If he leaves his cigarette burning in an ashtray, she must put it out before it sets the tablecloth afire.

When he tries to attack her, she must evade him gracefully and without aspersion to his virility. Then, if she is married to him, she it is who gets up the next morning while her dashing consort of the night before lies prostrate on the bed nursing a death rattle. Never, never, must she expect any show of remorse the next day; she will be far more apt to hear him proudly prating to his friends: "I really got pissed last night! Oh, boy! I can't remember a thing from the time we left Tony's" And this in the same smug tone he would use to announce a hole-in-one.

Well, the hell with it. Any woman drinker who made such a mess of herself as men usually do, would be about as popular as a Black Widow spider. When you think what a woman has to put up with when she goes out to hoist a few with her beloved, it's a wonder that she ever bothers. Except, of course, she really can manage to have a little fun after he passes out, or before her own cirrhosis of the liver sets in.

Who was that Gent I saw You with Last Night?

GILLIAN REYNOLDS

I'VE just come to tell you about the husband. He's gone back to his wife. He has, straight. Don't laugh too hard, ladies, we're in a very old building.

But seriously though, my father-in-law now, I wouldn't say he's mean. But the moths in his wallet are on time-and-a-half. Mind you, he's not so bad when you get to know him. No, he's not such a bad old skin. Bought me a drink the other week and only charged me four pence on the glass.

Going for your tea at my father-in-law's is like Fred Emney in a kilt . . . not enough to go around. But posh, he's definitely posh. Dead posh he is, my father-in-law. He even drinks his tea with a knife and fork.

But seriously though, ladies, I wish you could meet the husband . . . lovely little fellow he is. I wouldn't say he was small. No, I wouldn't say he was small. But next to him Jimmy Clitheroe looks like Charlton Heston. Never mind Charlton Heston—he makes Wee Georgie Wood look like bloody Tarzan.

It was his birthday last week. Aah! Lovely little fellow he is, straight. I'd do anything for him, and I'd better, his father made me put it in writing. So it's his birthday, and I gave him this nice new tie, only trouble . . . he tripped over it and broke his bleedin' arm.

Shame that, cos it matched his nice new suit. Lovely suits he's got. Irish tweed they are. Don't show the Guinness stains. Has them specially made for him by the leprechauns. I almost cried, I did, honest, the day he went into long pants.

But seriously though, I had a terrible experience with him the other day. The cleaning lady put him up on the bloody mantelpiece, with the other ornaments. She did, straight. Took him three hours to get down. He made it in the end, though, he bloody did. He hung on to the clock hands and waited till it got to half past six. Smashing little fellow. Eight pints of beer and he was right as rain.

He can get a bit nasty though when he's been drinking. Bottle of cherry brandy and he's away. Threatened to take on the pub cat the other night so they told me. Honest, that's what they said. Mind you, I think it was the mouse put him up to it.

We never fight though. Never. The day we were married he said to me, he did, "My darling, if I ever raise my voice to you, may I be struck dumb, dearest." And he never has. Never to this day. His fist, his foot, his little shillelagh. But never his voice. He stood on the chair the other day. Going to hit me, he was. Seriously, he gave me knee one hell of a tap with the tea spoon. Flew into a rage then. Said he was leaving. He did. Said he was leaving me, soon as he saved up the bus fare. Shouldn't take him long, he still goes on a scholar's.

Comes in useful that. Gets in half price at the pictures and all. Loves the pictures, he does. Seen *Snow White and the Seven Dwarfs* thirty-six times. He came back from *Butch Cassidy and the Sundance Kid* the other day and spent the rest of the week trying to ride his tricycle in slow motion.

But seriously though, ladies, my husband's a marvellous provider, a marvellous provider. Straight that is We have a marvellous little home. Small it is. Well, I wouldn't say it was small. Crowded is more like it. Listen, our house is so little every time we make any noise the mice bang on the wall.

But the husband, he's not a bit like his brother. No, he's not a bit like his brother. Their Frank, big fat fellow he is. Well, not so much fat as huge, even his razor's on time-and-a-half. Gets his suits made at Cammell Lairds does their Frank. Loves his grub, their Frank does. Loves chips, a sack

"We're reconciled . . . this morning he called me a cow."

132

of spuds does him twice. You should see his dinner, they bring a Shell tanker up the Mersey to pour the gravy on. But his table manners, they're dead shockin'. Disgusting. You know what I mean—he makes Desperate Dan look like the bloody Galloping Gourmet.

Works in a zoo, Frank does. If the elephant's not feeling well, they just bung him in the cage and no one notices the difference. Well, it's his nose you see. Long. Well, not so much long as enormous. When he gets a cold the germs are on time-and-a-half. Blew his nose the other day, he did, and everyone thought it was the Concorde.

My husband—the little fellow—and their Frank. They love a round of golf. Great game, golf. Like a golf joke, do you? Aah! Wait a minute though. I saw an awful sad thing the other day, I did. There was this Irishwoman, a Scotch-woman, a Welshwoman, and a Pakistani lady out playing a morning foursome, and they're on the twelfth.

Long drive the twelfth is. Four hundred and five yards down to the green with two sand bunkers and the old tram-yards standing in your way. You know the hole, runs right alongside the cemetery road opposite the Co-op jam factory. Beautiful day it was. These four girls really enjoying them-selves. Just got off the night shift, and straight out for a round. Nothing like it, well, almost nothing.

Down there on their second shot, two hundred yards up to the green, use a number five iron on that myself. Ought to get there in two, one putt and you're away for a birdie. Great. Nothing like it, well, almost nothing. Just then a funeral procession goes by. Well, right away the girls stop playing. Stand there, you know, dead respectful. Blodwen even took her fag out. When it's gone by, they go to play on. But Fiona's still standing there. Stood standing she is, head down, tears in her eyes. "Eh, Fiona," says Bernadette, "play on." "Aye," says Fiona, "but he was a good husband to me." Think about it, think about it. You're coughing well tonight.

Now in a minute, I'm going to ask you to welcome a great little novelty act. It's his first time in this club and in fact he's only been in show business two weeks—since the Co-op soap factory went on short time. I know you're going to enjoy Bert Parkinson (that's only his stage name, of course), a great little exotic dancer, all the way from Chorlton-cum-Hardy. I want to tell you, what he does with a cobra is nobody's business. And don't forget, next week we've got another great bill lined up. Four singers, Alf Parkinson at the piano, and a top line comedienne, direct from the telly, Sarah Jane Parkinson (that's only her stage name, naturally). Free hot pot, Tia Maria ninepence a pint.

You've been a great audience, ladies. Really great. Let me know where you're working tomorrow night and I'll come round and watch you.

FIONA MacCARTHY
Calls for
Equal Rights
in Eating

I LIKE eating in restaurants alone. Or anyway, I know that I'd enjoy it if by chance I was a man. I'd appreciate the way the waiter led me to my table, in the centre of the room, with such politeness and respect; I'd choose my meal contentedly and flutter through the wine list, selecting a half-bottle of quite distinguished claret, and maybe read a book and maybe simply sit and contemplate. If I was a man I'd have a happy, peaceful time.

But as I am a woman, all these pleasures are impossible. We call ourselves emancipated, yet the fact remains that women eating out alone are at a disadvantage. So much so that one is almost regarded as a freak. I know because I often have to do it when I'm working; I know the ins and outs of it, the nuances and subtleties, from very early breakfasts to last sittings in the dining-room, all designed to make a woman absolutely miserable. Often, one is very nearly driven to retreat.

Surprise; sheer disapproval; a strange commiseration ("Poor dear, it's sad to see a woman eating by herself''): any, or sometimes all, of these emotions greet you at the entrance to the dining-room or restaurant. Head waiters in the grand hotels I find the most disdainful. But the dreadfullest of all are smiling ladies in black dresses who show you to your table in department stores at lunchtime. They give displays of sympathy: "Just one? Well, wait a minute and I'll find you a nice table." They make you stand aside as they usher in their parties of women two by two or four by four (all hatted for a festive day in town) and then, if single men come in, they preen themselves and lead them to the tables by the window, and then remember me.

Any man who thinks I am exaggerating ought to dress up as a woman and go out to a restaurant where he is used to being given the best table, and see how they dispose of him. I almost guarantee that, if his disguise is in any degree adequate, he will be shown to the most inconspicuous corner: the table in the nook behind the pillar, or the table in what used to be the cupboard at the bottom of the stair, in the very smallest horse-box (in an equestrian restaurant), the table (in a fish one) behind the tank of trout. And if you complain that it is draughty, cramped or viewless, you will certainly be told it is the best available, the implication being that a solitary woman is not a much-loved customer and takes what she can get.

Prepare for a long wait. Or, almost worse, prepare for waiters who insist upon your order the minute you sit down, giving you no time for gentle reading of the menu (which is one of the great joys, in my view, of eating out). The rude impatient attitude to women on their own shows clearly what extraordinary prejudice still lasts; an almost puritanical point-of-view persists that women by themselves can have no interest in food. Gastronomy is smiled on in the solitary man, but a woman who embarks on a discussion of the menu is made to feel a glutton. I am speaking from experience. This hint of a reproach is the result of the belief that women are born home-bodies and should not be out gallivanting.

Mutter, mutter, mutter, go the waiters—I can hear them—if I ask for just a glass of very ordinary wine. (They would pour me out two carafes, thinking nothing of it, if my husband had been there to drink it with me. Why is this?) Mutter, mutter, mutter, go the people sitting round me: "what is *she* doing here alone? and look, she's got a wedding ring." They launch into discussions, phrases of which hit me, on present-day morality and marrying too young.

With much the same ideas of female immorality or, to put it at its kindest, the hope of making friends, people come and talk to a solitary woman, in a restaurant or airport lounge or even in the Ritz. Once or twice I have not minded, when the men were interesting. But usually they are the most intolerable bores. Their idea of conversation for a gallivanting woman sends one running, with relief, for the next plane or train back home, or rushing to the Ladies' Room, or desperately waving to the waiter for one's bill—and will he get a taxi quickly?

This has all gone on too long. If women on their own are so vulnerable, surely this must be a female fault. We should maybe be much ruder and much tougher and more arrogant. In fact, we should probably behave much more like men, not only for the sake of the people who (as I am) are sometimes on their own for a day or two, but also for spinsters and widows and women who from reasons of accident or choice, are often solitary. They could have a nicer time—and not be so open to misinterpretation—if women as a whole could put head waiters in their place.

Now that women have been voting for fifty years, wear trousers, and seem to be achieving equal pay for equal work, equal rights with men to the best table in the Mirabelle or British Railways dining cars should not be out of reach.

"She'd like to see some rings."

The
Wedding Industry

THELWELL

"Here it comes! Bridegroom hasn't turned up, can we make

"That looks great! Now, what do you fancy for your bridesmaids?"

"I see you picked the same caterers as last time, dear."

reductions?"

"That was lovely! Could you hold him up just once more?"

"How quickly can you do invitations?"

"It's from my ex-husband. An automatic toast scraper."

"Have you any ready-sliced?"

Can Alan Brien slave over a hot stove all day and still find true happiness?

St. Valentine's Day guide to the future of marriage

IF that title sounds a bit sensational, fellas, it's strictly international. Remember there are a million more men between the ages of 15 and 50 than there are women—so every gal has her choice today and many of them are getting very choosy. Since equal pay made them the wage earners in the majority of homes, it behooves us housemales to get up off our floppy Y-fronts, slip into something truly masculine, and fight back against those single guys out there who are only too eager to share our breadwinners.

Now, though we've too long been embarrassed by our manly modesty to admit it, every chap is at heart a gigolo. And the time has come for us to let it all hang out. To use all those tricks of the trade perfected by our bachelor brothers to keep married women on their hook when they stray from our hearth. Let's be honest, men, what do you think of when you hear the word "housemale"? You picture somebody more like a father than a lover whose only sartorial decision is whether to wear his belt above or below his comfortable pot belly. You think of somebody with spectacles on his forehead, dandruff on his collar, nicotine on his fingers, soup on his flies, and five o'clock shadow at nine in the morning. He couldn't arouse a nipple in the randiest milkwoman.

Take off your clothes and stand in front of the mirror—it doesn't look so much like flesh, as like a suit of old-fashioned combinations left yellowing too long in a bottom drawer. Would you truly like any other woman, except your wife, to see you like that? You don't need to be a graduate-housemale, though many of us are these days, to see the advantage of behaving like a gigolo which is, let's face it, what the male secretary at your wife's office often seems to be. And, don't forget, when she goes off on her business trips, or working weekends, unscrupulous firms will make sure that she doesn't lack for masculine "companionship" in the evenings.

Being a gigolo isn't all sexual attractiveness, but one of the reasons your wife may be tempted to acquire one is that she is not getting enough at home. (Sorry to be so crude, boys, but we all know that a red-blooded truly womanly woman at some time or another is only interested in one thing. An erogenous zone has no conscience—and nature gave them more than us.) There is no such animal as a completely impotent man. If you think you are desirable, you will feel desire. Many of us are not frigid, we're just *unawakened*.

Don't let her find you coming to the door in clothes more appropriate to her sex—sweater and jeans. Dress up in something that even the trendiest and most exhibitionist male young thing would hesitate to wear at work, something conjuring up the historic role of the man in the olden days. A good device is the costume we once used to kill in—hire a uniform with lots of gold braid, belts and shiny buttons and a cocked hat with feathers. She'll get a kick out of it if you could also carry a sword.

Or if that is not your style, and you are more of a modern lad, why not a jungle combat suit complete with pistol holster and strings of decorative hand-grenades? (Though, personally, I prefer these in sackcloth as nightwear. And here, do take care never to undress in her presence, except in a low light. What she thinks she's glimpsing is always more exciting than what she can't help seeing.) Many of my housemale friends tell me that hunting outfits also create the right impression—tweed plus-fours, or web leggings, leather patches on the shoulder and elbows, and a dog licking your boots for artificial blood stains.

There is nothing shameful in borrowing all the arts and crafts of the Casanova or the Don Juan. When you ring her up at the office to find if she's going to be late, or to remind her to bring back some wine for the dinner guests, use your deepest, sexiest voice and put in some heavy breathing when she breaks off to apologise for the interruption to her female colleagues. Pop an occasional loving, or even just a comical, note into her brief-case before she leaves—she may come across it just at the moment when she most needs to be reminded of your existence!

On birthdays and wedding anniversaries, don't always buy her something, buy a present that will make you more adorable and decorative—a new toupee in a colour you have never tried before, for instance, or a pipe which matches your eyes. At night, always make your toilet early on, perhaps when she's relaxing over the evening paper or in front of the TV, thus leaving the bathroom free for her at bedtime. Nothing is more frustrating and off-putting for a busy woman, after the stresses of the day, than having to hang around while you pluck the hairs in your nose or clean the wax out of your ears.

But don't skimp through fear of keeping her waiting—toe nails as well as finger nails, and under the arms is not the only spot for deodorant. But above all, *spoil her*. Lay out the bath towels, turn down the sheets, adjust the reading lamp in case she wants a last-minute run-through of the work she has brought home.

If she has any special interests that men traditionally are not expected to share—such as abortion, the arts, handicapped children, the developing countries, race prejudice or the like— try to show an intelligent concern. Take trouble to arrange the weekends so that she feels free to paint, or write novels, or attend demonstrations, or even go off for a night out with the girls without saying "but you've been with the girls all week".

But above all, make sure that your sex life is full and warm and lively, chaps, please. It may irritate you that women are so easily aroused, so selfishly dedicated to their own satisfactions, so ready to assume that you must always be eager and willing. Explain that you need time, and tenderness, and a display of affection as well as passion. Any intelligent woman will understand your difficulties if you manage to find the right tactful words. And if necessary, do not be ashamed to fake a climax so flattering to the female vanity. You need her more than she needs you.

"Same here . . . I tried the WVS and WI but found this much more fulfilling."

TOP SEX

GILLIAN TINDALL

THERE is a rumbling complaint that women writers moan too much about how awful it is being a woman. Myself, I think women moan too much, full stop.

What's more, their choice of subjects to moan about sometimes seems arbitrary, ill-related to the realities of their lives. The fact that women often suffer valiantly and privately the really awful things that happen to them (like widowhood, or no one wanting to marry them anyway) but complain loudly about other things, perhaps provides a clue: many women, of all intellectual levels, *enjoy* their martyrdom. They enjoy feeling victimised, particularly when the victimiser is seen as a man, or men. The obscure masochism which forms a part of even the most cheerful feminine sexual response translates itself, in more general terms, into a tendency for us to want to see ourselves as being peculiarly and femininely subject to the slings and arrows of outrageous fortune, slung in our direction by a "male-dominated society." ("Ooo—do it harder!")

In past generations there was a good solid reason for moaning: the pains, dangers, heart-breaks and lasting discomforts frequently inflicted by pre-anaesthetic, pre-antiseptic child-beds should never be under-estimated when considering the lives of our ancestors; the envious modern attitude which tends to see these women as "so secure" compared with us, their enlightened descendants, is surely a neo-sentimentality carried to the point of idiocy: what's *secure* in carrying a child whose birth you know may kill you? All the same . . . I bet that some of our great-grandmothers did actually get satisfaction too out of their very real suffering. Certainly some of them seem to have gone out of their way to court it, never saying no to dear Papa (or the Mister, according to class) encouraging him to behave like a monster of masterful selfishness when probably he would often have been amenable to a little quiet reason.

Today, when only the wilfully incompetent or very Catholic are permanent martyrs to their own fertility, new bases for moaning have had to be found, particularly in the middle classes where life, on the whole, is undeniably comfortable and controllable. Hence that great invention of the last decade, the Captive Wife, written about in the women's pages and colour-supplements of the posher papers, referred to in respectful asides by women novelists like me, who are themselves less captive than almost anyone else in society and mostly make damn sure they stay that way!

The typical Captive Wife, so runs the myth, is an intelligent [*sic*] graduate, who has married soon after leaving college (why?), has started a family before becoming established in any career (*why?*). Couldn't the Great Fulfilment of Motherhood have waited for two, three, or even five years? Most other achievements have to be waited for, after all. She has two, three, or even four children, and then discovers what you would think this clever girl could have foreseen from the outset—namely, that she is stuck at home with an occupation that does not fulfil her capacities and with no immediate prospect of getting out of it.

Naturally, she's not entirely happy. So she complains—about discrimination against women, about her "loss of identity," about how tired she feels and how difficult and at the same time oring her life is. (And I'm sure it is.) She may have a guilty wallow about not using her education—or she may (lots more opportunity for masochism here!) dump her children, get a job and then carry on about how guilty she feels because she's *not* staying at home all day any longer. Pundits will tell her she must work/she mustn't work, she is a ghastly failure/she is marvellous—but the one thing, it seems, that no one, not even her long-suffering husband is supposed to say is "Come off it, love. You brought it on yourself. It's your life, your choices. Every choice, for both sexes, has its compensation and its disadvantages. You have an income: mine, and time: your own. Do whatever you think best, but STOP MOANING."

Meanwhile, what about this husband, tied week in week out to his exciting, stimulating (or is it?) job, for which *he* has probably had to work and plan and think ahead, or else, travelling for hours every day in the rush hour, with three weeks off a year and no breaks or kudos for having babies? What about the crushing mortgage he has had to take on to house the idyll of family life his wife once thought was all she wanted? What about *his* frustrations, his conflicts, tensions and disappointments at work, his sacrifices, his fragmented identity? What about a few sympathetic, sensitive, probing, colour-features on the Captive Husband, then? Any offer?

For the Woman who has given everything

JONATHAN ROUTH

NEIMAN-MARCUS are at it again. Last year the Dallas, Texas, store was encouraging the rich woman customer at whom its Christmas catalogue is directed to give His and Hers midget submarines. A previous year it was Islands. This year's catalogue woos her to spend $18,000 on gliders for friends—no, wait a minute, the gliders fitted with turbo-jets and costing $32,000 are for friends, the gliders proper ("the world's most sophisticated soaring machine") are for the servants. Or she is wooed to invest a mere $3,000 (exclusive of sculptor's airfare) in life-size portable replicas of herself or her loved ones "programmed to laugh as long as you like at your jokes or say yes in any language you choose at the touch of a remote control button. Specify seated or standing model." (—And I'd also specify, if I was as careful with my money as undoubtedly Nieman-Marcus' rich woman customer is, that the sculptor economised by gliding to the appointment.)

I wonder if this Neiman-Marcus gimmick will catch on? Instead of the signed photo in the silver frame on the grand piano, the life-size replica: the Queen Mother, Liberace, Cousin Willy, the Provost of Kings, old Nanny Blad. Your drawing room is going to look terribly full. And the noise, when you press the remote-control buttons and they all start laughing and jabbering in their different languages.

My complaint is that Neiman-Marcus don't go far enough or think big enough in their yearly search for a new novelty that the rich woman can give to commemorate her richness. After all, why stop at Islands when there are whole countries available?

Darling, I've a surprise for you!

Can't guess . . .

Begins with a "T".

Not another Titian?

No darling—Tibet!

Or, of course, she might have had it gift-wrapped for you:

Dear Cousin Laura,

It was ever so thoughtful of you to give me Tibet for Christmas—just exactly what I've always wanted. Hope by now you'll have received Ethiopia safely and get a bundle of laughs out of it.

Well, a country isn't all that far removed from the ultimate present that, I submit, the rich woman of discernment and imagination could really give. After all, she should be looking for something unique. It's not nice to know that maybe 100 other people have received gliders this Christmas. So I suggest People. Not Neiman-Marcus replica people, but real people People.

I quote from next year's Neiman-Marcus catalogue (the request on your Order Form to "specify Colour" has, of course, a discreet little sticker over it referring to contraventions of the Race Act in this country):

87. The TRUDGES, Mr. Arthur C. and Mrs. Ethel M. (circa 1910). This is a unique English pair at present in the Collection of Stockport Corporation where they are displayed as part-time slipper-bath keepers. He quotes Longfellow continuously while she whistles Wagner. (Not guaranteed.)
... £120.00 the pair

88. PREEN, Miss Alison (1956). A Staffordshire lady in mint condition. ... £4,000.00

89. CONNOISSEUR'S CROWD (A Collection of 12 Persons). Each Crowd is guaranteed to contain at least Three Toadies, skilled in grovelling, forelock-pulling and lickspittling. Two False Flatterers with abject expressions and inferior presences; and one small middle-aged female adept at giving Adoring Looks. The rest of a Connoisseur's Crowd is made up of Assorted People as in stock (state preference for Male or Female). ... £30,000.00

90. (From the Antique and Rare Persons Dept.) DEVREAUX, Lt.-Col. Sir Abelard. This magnificent specimen dating from the end of the Victorian era, with his unstoppable flow of military anecdotes, makes a fine centre-piece to a dinner-table. (Guaranteed for 18 months only.) ... £6,000.00

91. A SET (6) of Venetian Pickpockets. These hardy little fellows will require no looking after at all and are guaranteed to provide hours of mirth and homely fun every day ... £12,000.00

Of course, it's just possible that more firms than Neiman-Marcus would become interested in stocking this line. In which case we might expect:

"Bargains in Slightly-worn and Secondhand People at the C & C Surplus Stores. Choose your Person from the Widest Selection of People in Town."

"We can supply any sort of person in the World—Everyone from a Midget to a Throng at Whiteleys."

"This week it's Scotch Week in Harrods People Department —your chance to acquire a Genuine Kilted Crofter, a high Highlander or Haggis-eating Hebridean. Take a Person home with you today!"

I somehow feel it's terribly unlikely though. And it doesn't help either in deciding what to give the Rich Woman in return for whatever fabulous gift, Person or not, she's given you or me.

I'm just seeing if Neiman-Marcus have any suggestion to make. Here we are. "$10 and Under". (Rather common for N-M to have such a section I feel.) "A silver metal shopping bag to fill with cigarettes." No, I don't think she'd want to be seen smoking out of a shopping bag. "All-purpose Italian knife with blade, file, screwdriver." No, she's not planning on being in prison. "A Napoleonic Bee."—I doubt if she's got one of those. I doubt if anyone has. What is it? What does it do? Never mind. It costs $5.50. She shall have it.

Or else a 10p tin-opener from the local friendly hardware store which I'll bet she actually needs in her kitchen.

"The black Wedgwood! Some relative of cook's must have passed away."

On Leap Year Day 1972 Barbara Castle and fifteen other distinguished women (see below) had lunch with the Editor to talk about a woman's issue of Punch. Hors d'oeuvre was getting through a picket line of Women's Lib protesting against Punch's Wednesday all-male lunch. To sort out the pros and cons, we threw our pages open to Gillian Reynolds (who was at the lunch) and Stanley Reynolds (who was at home baby-sitting).

GILLIAN REYNOLDS

JUST because you may have seen me at a party busy prising the best-looking man in the room apart from the best-looking woman, don't run off with the idea that I'm some sort of a fanatic about sexual apartheid. Since the best-looking man on these occasions is usually my husband it's a fair bet that somewhat special feelings have been aroused by a particular instance of sexual co-existence rather than any fanatic zeal on my part.

In general, in fact, I approve of men and women enjoying each other's company. Furthermore, I endorse totally professional and private competition between the sexes at all levels. The thought of men becoming secretaries, chars, and station buffet attendants while women take over the Stock Exchange, the Cabinet and the Church of England is one to make race the pulses of any redblooded graduate wife.

On equal pay, mortgage rights, hire purchase responsibilities and the right to look like a slob if you want to, I am a vocal enthusiast for women's rights. If a daughter of mine wanted to take up being a jockey, I'd pause only in my blessing to point out that there's probably more future in being a bookie. If life allotted her a less glamorous slot, like being a bin-man, one would have to rejoice that equality of opportunity was at least reaching beyond the professions.

Where I part company with militant feminists is on the "right to assemble and get up to mono-sexual tomfoolery" issue. If men want to have clubs where only men can go, why should I stop them? As long as they're going there to eat, sleep, and read the papers, I'll let someone else do the cooking, the picking up of the debris and the listening to the snores with a light heart. If women enjoy organising themselves into lunch clubs where you pay two pounds for the chance to eat grilled chicken wings and listen to a speaker recall the lighter side of the Civil Service, who am I to say nay?

It is said that men have not welcomed women into certain areas of their recreational lives since this would impose undue restraints on the language used therein. Indeed, I have heard the opinion that what has barred women contributors from taking an equal place at the hallowed Punch table has been the chance that the odd "damn" or "bloody" dropping from the lips of a male wit might bring blushes of shame to female cheeks. This argument proceeds to the assumption that the restraints thus inevitably placed on the conversation would be such as to staunch all further flow of bons mots, epigrams, and saucy stories.

Without going into realistic details about what gets written on the walls of the girls' changing-rooms (since I find this is the sort of thing that makes men blush and when they do that I lose the thread of the limericks) I might propose that the middle class male idea of "girl talk" is not the whole picture. I might call in evidence the annual banquets held by the ladies of St. John's Retail Market in Liverpool, the first one of which I remember as if it were seventeen years ago.

The event was held in the private room of a downtown restaurant and the only men present were the band. Ada Stubbs, my mother's girlhood friend, a poulterer of prime repute and the most brilliant raconteuse to grace the market flagstones, sat drinking boiler-makers of cherry brandy and Guinness. At eleven o'clock a roll on the drums announced the cabaret, a cross between a carnival parade, a satirical pageant and a choreographic parody, in which most com-

"It'll be a sort of wine and cheese party except there'll be coffee instead of wine."

148

mon varieties of male folly, female weakness and human grotesquerie were held up for ribald comment which, I need not add, flowed as readily as the tears of laughter from our eyes. Only the band blushed.

On another level entirely, where would the country be without Women's Institutes, federations of university women, mono-sexual religious and political groups, and Old Girls' institutions? If we are still living in times where people find it easier to organise themselves on gender lines, so be it. If men want to keep me out of certain pubs, Press Clubs, and dining societies, that's their loss. If they let me in I'd probably talk too loud, swear too much and end up running the place.

That certainly doesn't mean I'm about to run off and organise a group of "Ladies in . . .", "Girls for . . .", or "Women's . . .". The occasional company of one's own sex can be a joy and a solace, but beyond that I am not prepared to go. Groups where *everyone* is competing to be Head Girl leave me as cold as the ones where middle-aged men indulge in ersatz camaraderie and phony ritual. But if you want to do it, go right ahead. I'm off after the best-looking man in the room.

"*. . . and you call those hands clean!*"

YOU will never know how hard it is for me to write this. I am telling my story not for the money. Money means nothing to me now. In my heady heyday hovering high in what our sick society calls . . . a man's world I had money. And all the things it can buy. But can money buy you happiness? Can money buy you the love of a good woman? Yes, it can . . . where was I? Oh yes . . .

DEEDEE MORTON'S PLAYTHING

You will never know how hard it is for me to write this story of how I became . . . the plaything of the Former DeeDee Morton.

DISGUSTING RITUALS

To give you some idea of how hard it is for me to confess to being a traitor to his sex, I have been working on that first paragraph for two and a half days now pausing only to scrub floors, cook meals, perform disgusting rituals with a bucket of dirty nappies in the secrecy of our so-called scullery, and cry out, "No" and "My God! No!" and "Not knives!!!" at a curly-headed two-year-old who, as the hours pass by, begins to bear a more and more amazing resemblance to the Former DeeDee Morton's brother.

"I don't think you've quite caught the point of wife swapping parties, Mr. Beresford."

GOMORRAH???

I will not offend the ears of unmarried girls with disgusting details of my sordid life. Instead I will tell you how *any* life is preferable to my former one, the life of the male chauvinist pig world. Sodom and Gomorrah on the expense account. (By the way, I'm pretty clear on Sodom but what exactly went on in Gomorrah?) Blue stories in the Men Only bar at the Cricket Club, what really happened at . . . and my God! He's opened the washing machine door on a Number Two Programme wash (high temperature wash—whites and colour-fast cottons and linens).

THE POINT

There must be a point to this piece? I knew there was one around here somewhere when I started.

OH YES

Oh yes. Mention all chaps together to me and it's not nights on foaming pints and japes around the dart board that come to mind. It's little Ambrose, littler Alexander, and littlest Abel and foaming buckets of dirty nappies that spring to mind.

TRIXIE AND DOLORES

Sure, I've still got a full head of hair on my chest. Sure, I used to be a two fisted reporter. I used to punch a clock and collect Luncheon Vouchers. I used to show Trixie and Dolores a good time. But I was a stranger to my boys. (You've seen Spencer Tracy in *Edward, My Son.* You've seen Broderick Crawford make a bum out of John Derek in *All the King's Men.* What was needed around here was a touch of the Fred McMurray's, a touch of the Jimmy Stewart's.)

THE BROADS

What good is expense account world travel, first class hotels, silk shirts, mohair suits, a passport to adventure, and having to beat the broads off with a stick if you're a stranger to your boys? Put it another way, the Former DeeDee Morton went out to work and someone always gets left with the nappies. Look at it this way: I am sitting at a brand new six-foot long gleaming white kitchen table which was bought by the Former DeeDee Morton and scratch it again, kid, with that biro and I'll twist your other arm.

TRIXIE AND DOLORES AGAIN

We would not have this beautiful new table to drive me insane trying to keep little Alexander from scratching it if the Former DeeDee Morton did not go out and compete in the masculine world of big shoulders, double whiskies, expense account travel, Havana cigars, silk shirts . . . a high powered, go-girl of the '70s, stepping into a man's role, showing

Trixie and Dolores a good time while I sit at home writing lyric poems and listening to the music of the spheres and the Number Two wash overflowing.

BETWEEN CLEAN SHEETS

But if anyone asks me what I think of sexual apartheid (and the Editor did or at least he asked the Former DeeDee Morton to ask me and she left a hastily scrawled note on the kitchen blackboard—clean sheets, eat ham today or will go bad, woollens in Number Five wash, sexual apartheid, back Thursday, two extra Pintas) I don't have to think twice.

THE CRUX

But the point, Stanley. Oh, yes, the crux of the matter. Our little life here in Liverpool's Sefton Park is the maddest dream of Women's Lib come true. I sit and watch the nappies spin dry while the Former DeeDee Morton struggles in a man's world. This month, the Former DeeDee Morton appears on *PM* talking about the Budget ("as an ordinary housewife" Bill Hardcastle said). Then she will sky to New York for a week to corner the market in wheat or something.

TRIXIE AND DOLORES

I can't speak for other house drudges. But when I get a day off, burning a brassiere is not my idea of a good time. Neither is clubbing together with members of my own sex for an evening around the dart board. Just sit me down in a nice restaurant and let someone else do the washing up for a change. The problem of course is getting Trixie and Dolores to pick up the bill. Women's Lib still has a long way to go.

"I'd like something vaguely repellent, please."

"I've just *aad* this wonderful dream . . . I was being chased through a protected Green Belt by the Minister for the Environment."

Anything We Can Do They Can Do Better

The traditional male domination of expense account entertaining is now being challenged by the new breed of high powered women executives, who, as MAHOOD shows, have a natural talent for it.

"Of course I love you, Miss Bradbury—haven't I ordered ten times more sprocket mouldings than we know what to do with?"

*"**Personally** I always take a little nap after lunch."*

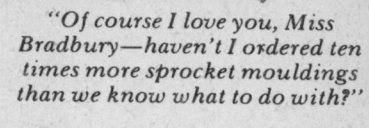

*"I'm sorry, gentlemen, Company rules, orgies are only for **export** customers."*

"It's a present for a very old customer— would you have something containing monkey glands?"

*"Good Heavens, Miss Opie, I wasn't expecting **round the clock** talks."*

"Now, remember, when you see me produce the contract, give 'September Song' everything you've got."

' You poor dear, has that Amalgamated woman been pressurizing you again?'

"Sixty-seven! You're joking, I've never seen a businessman in such a magnificent state of preservation."

The Women of Europe

*An authoritative survey of
the ladies of the EEC
by ALAN COREN*

THE FRENCHWOMAN

THE Frenchwoman proper, if that's the word, began in 1914, when she took to bathing in mill streams behind the lines, and leaping up and down in the water, waving at Lew Ayres and Slim Somerville, and mouthing, through bee-sting lips, such eternal verities as "Wot 'ave you done wiz my cloze, you naughty Tommee?"

When the war was ended, the Frenchwoman got out of the water, lashed herself into her waspie, and went back to sitting behind an estaminet till, from which fortification (she kept the keys between her breasts, an indulgence she allowed to nothing else) she ruled the family with an iron rod, called the franc. Her daughters remained chaste until 1925, when the first wave of young American novelists struck the country, whose need for first-hand material was such that by 1929, there were fewer than ten virgins in the entire country.

They held out until 1931.

During the latter 'thirties, so deftly chronicled by Renoir and Gabin, Frenchwomanhood was rigidly trifurcated: they were either (1) dressed in berets and fishnet stockings and thrown through the windows of the darker nightclubs, still smoking, or (2) married to Adolphe Menjou whose own impeccably clad assignations (he is rumoured to have worn tails in bed) forced them into one passionate affair with a frail bronchitic pianist that ended in the rain, or (3) living in such grey conurbations as Metz or Valenciennes where they became pregnant at the hands (and so forth) of Parisian travelling men with pencil moustaches who had a habit of shooting their cuffs and leaving their playmates to die in childbirth.

None of these women, i.e. all Frenchwomen, ever enjoyed sex at all. It was mainly a source of grief, frustration, and disillusionment. All it had was a thin edge over drinking alone.

The World War II years were somewhat better for the Frenchwoman, since she could either collaborate, in which case sex, however miserable, meant stockings, chocolate, sable, and riding around in a Mercedes; or she could work for the Maquis, which meant a lot of fresh air and cycling, and Doing It In A Good Cause, i.e. sleeping with RAF rear-gunners awaiting repatriation.

*"By gum, Mr. Tanaka, Japan's just like West Hartlepool! Women
don't count for much there either!"*

After 1945, Frenchwomanhood underwent (choosing one's
words carefully) a sexual revolution, in that enjoyment crept
into bed. In the Bardot years, busts got bigger, clothes came
off (pre-war, much of the sex-life of the Frenchwoman took
place in evening gowns, well-cut of course, but complex and
noisy), and men started looking like Belmondo and Delon,
instead of like brick outhouses in blue vests. Coyness
disappeared (the French, contrary to their winking, louche
image, have always had more sexual hang-ups than any race
on earth, with the possible exception of the Urak islanders,
who will only make love in shallow water, at night), and a
jolly good time was had by all.

All this came to an end with the *nouvelle vague*, a period,
starting in 1957, when Frenchwomen grew pitifully confused,
unable to distinguish between husbands and lovers, lovers
and lovers, and husbands and husbands. Most of the time they
wandered about on the terraces of the more decrepit castles,
trying to sort things out.

Of late, as you will have seen in the newspapers,
poisonings appear to have begun again, a bad sign. However,
another war might clear the air a bit. Frenchwomen seem to
thrive on wars.

THE LUXEMBOURGOISE

There are nine women in Luxembourg, and they are kept
pretty busy making stamps. It is not the smallest female
population in Europe: there are only eight women in
Monaco, five in Andorra, and Frau Ingrid Hofmeister in
Liechtenstein. The Luxembourgoises are of middle height,
with the small, deft fingers of trained perforators, and all
look rather alike, except for Tante Marie, who has a wall-eye,

the inaccuracy of which restricts her activities to gumming.

Sexually, their lives are somewhat limited, there being only six men in the Grand Duchy, and not too many places to hide; in fact, there is only one eligible bachelor, Armand Arfamault, and one copse, so that he is kept pretty busy. He is also attacked by incensed husbands with pitiable regularity, and being too tired ever to defend himself, is growing less and less eligible with each passing night.

Given these extreme spatial limitations, the Luxembourgoise is sadly cut off from many of the thrills which her European sisters enjoy: not for her the dirty weekends (anyone attempting to pass themselves off as M. et Mme. Smeeth is unlikely to fool the other thirteen inhabitants), not for her the regular hot afternoon trysts (Armand Aframault being available, at best, one afternoon in nine, and then only when his work as an album-binder is over for the day), not for them the billets-doux slipped to milkmen in the empty bottle (the entire population lives in one small block of flats, and shares the step), not for them the heady escape to mountain retreat or country cottage (there is only one mountain in Luxembourg; it is some eight feet higher than the rest of the country, bare as an egg, and commands an uninterrupted view of the only cottage, some six yards away).

It is hardly surprising, then, that the romantic life of the Luxembourgoise is spasmodic, fraught, and unfulfilled. She is, in consequence a dour and unrewarding mistress.

THE FRAU(LEIN)

It was Bismarck who welded the German woman into a fighting unit. Until the 1870's, she was a disparate collection of conflicting characteristics: buxom, flaxen peasant wench; brooding saga-heroine given to liaisons with owls and dragons and headless horsemen; fierce earth-mother waggoning her children from dukedom to dukedom, dirndled and parthenogenetic; randy noblewoman in the habit of savaging booted lieutenants on the sideboard; melancholy riparian songstress; and single-breasted artiste of the sabre.

It is not to be wondered at, therefore, that the German woman emerges in the early twentieth century as a figure in a top hat, black tights and a baritone voice, with a penchant for lashing out with a stockwhip and seeing, at the same time, that the boys in the backroom want for nothing. She is currently seen at her best upon the Reeperbahn (pronounced, for reasons which become obvious at Number 122b, second floor, Raperbahn), where for a small consideration, she will wrestle in mud, spit rivets through sheet ply, and perform a number of interesting tricks with ordinary household objects, like men. Beyond the Reeperbahn, German womanhood has undergone the well-known *Frauleinswunder*, indistinguishable in essence from the equally famous *Wirtschaftswunder*, in that it merely means that they are bigger and stronger than you are. Provided you stay away from mud, however, this need not be to your disadvantage, but take a friend along. They are also the most sexually liberated women in Europe, which is fine, since it keeps them from marching on the Sudetenland; what happens to the New German Woman when society channels her vigour into alternative areas may be seen from a glance at her East German *Schwester*, whose energy manifests itself in terrifying ways; unless you happen to like hanging around girls who can chuck a hammer into the next county, that is.

Connoisseurs of such things say that the German woman reached her apogee (often several times a week) in the last days of Weimar, when the decadence was so thick you could slice it like knackwurst, and everything went, including, unfortunately, the mark, with all that that entailed. It is worth remembering, therefore, for anyone with residual doubts about the economic stability of the EEC, that there is always a bright side to German inflation.

THE DUTCHWOMAN

The Dutchwomen fall into two quite distinct physical types: the small, corpulent, redfaced Edams, and the thinner, paler, larger Goudas. Having evolved underwater, the Dutchwoman is, perhaps, a trifle less hotblooded than other European ladies, but this is more than made up for by her expertise on the bicycle, an invaluable instrument for getting away quietly at night.

Which cannot be said for the clog.

"I thought there was a dock strike on here!"

There are one or two drawbacks to more serious and longer liaisons with Dutchwomen, prime among which is the fact that Queen Juliana is the richest woman in the world and her less elevated countrywomen have not been slow to see the advantages of the folding stuff. Couple this to a healthy appetite (for food) and a blasé attitude towards flowers (sick of tulips and their ilk, the Dutchwoman will rarely be satisfied with anything less than orchids or long-stemmed roses out of season), and you will observe that anyone with an overdraft should step warily upon embarking at the Hook.

Some of these stumbling-blocks may be overcome, however, by getting the ladies drunk on advocaat, a drink made from lawyers.

LA BELGE

Everything that the Belgian woman is has come about as a direct result of Belgium's being the most densely populated country in Europe. A woman for whom her native agronomists developed the sprout, this being the largest cabbage a busy housewife could possibly manoeuvre through the packed Brussels streets, will accept almost anything. It is those same teeming roads, crammed buses and trams, and general nose-to-ear social conditions that have made her so sexually sophisticated; since a lifetime of being wedged up against men on public transport has left her with few naiveties.

The obverse of this otherwise encouraging coin is that it is practically impossible to get her alone. With nary a spare millimetre of soil between Ostend and Liege, the chance of achieving a rendezvous is extremely remote: arrive thirty seconds late at the appointed spot, and you will find that your date has been shuffled on by the crowd, to be lost forever (they tend to fetch up eventually at the German border, weeping; which makes Aachen the lugubrious place it is, except for the week in the year when they throw their *Witzfest,* and God knows they need it).

THE ITALIAN WOMAN

Ninety-eight per cent of Italian women go around in black bombazine; it is the two per cent who go around without it with whom we should concern ourselves here.

Little was known about Italian women until 1951, when the first of them was spotted, standing in a rice field with a wisp of hair blowing into her incredible velvet eyes, and her dress tucked into her knickers. Since then, we have never looked back; except, of course, when driving too fast past rice fields. Sadly, the ubiquitous pasta has seen to it that rice remains a minor crop; despite the general feeling that if the entire country were put onto a rice economy, it would be no bad thing. The other villainy wrought by pasta is entirely dietetic: the beautiful, lissome, delectable Signorina of nineteen, can, in the space of a few short years (or, to put it another way, thirty-eight tons of fettucine) become an unbeautiful, unlissome, undelectable Signora beneath whom many a gondola has sunk like a brick, raising the water level to disastrous heights and threatening, very soon, to turn Venice into nothing more than a campanile or two poking above the surrounding silt.

The grafting of the Lollobrigidas, Lorens, Cardinales and so forth onto the cultural tapestry of the most sin-conscious country in Europe has done nothing for domestic calm, and foreign visitors should tread with care: visiting women may be turned, in an hour or so, into a mass of bluish-black bumps by frustrated local fingers, while visiting men, surrounded by the busty untouchables with which the landscape is dotted, may, in the same period, end up as holloweyed, dry-mouthed wrecks. The introduction of divorce a year or so ago should not be taken as an encouraging sign, since the traditional customs prevail: international brotherhood is one thing, but international Brotherhood is something very different, and one of the things known to mar a night of unbridled passion in Italy is a knock on the door in the small hours heralding the arrival of a brace of Cosa Nostra members. Cosa Nostra means "our thing", and good luck to it; but when they do their thing to you, and it becomes your thing, and medical science shakes its head and walks away, you may well find yourself asking whether Italy shouldn't ban the production of rice altogether.

SCANDINAVIA

At the time of going to press, the women of Scandinavia were uncertain about entry. They fall, therefore, outside the scope of this survey, if they fall anywhere.

One Out, The Lot Out

Turkish prostitutes having formed their own trade union—the Personal Service Workers' Union—one is tempted to wonder precisely what form their industrial action might take in the event of the failure of negotiations, say, or the difficulty of reaching a satisfactory conclusion after frank and free approaches from both sides. Would a go-slow not, in fact, work to their own disadvantage as well as play into the management's hands? Could a work-to-rule not involve them in such difficult situations as actually having to give massage, act, pose in front of cameras, or seek interesting secretarial positions? As for withdrawing labour . . . still, it's heartening for all good unionists to see one more example of private enterprise coming to terms with solidarity on the shop-floor.

"I've never known real kindness—except, of course, from soap powders."

My Mother-in-Law, She's That Fat, She's That Fat...

No, listen, there was this magazine called Punch, see, and the fellas there said hang on a minute, why don't we ring up all those star-studded professional comics, like you see on the telly and that, and ask them for the best (and the worst) of the gags that they've heard on mother-in-law, eh? So they did, see, and these comics said ...

Les Dawson

Funny you should ask. She was round the other night, my mother-in-law, knocked on the door. I knew it was her because next door's savage alsatian was whimpering. Not only that, our tortoise had got a For Sale notice on his shell. Any road, I opened the door before she broke it and she was stood there in the pouring rain, wearing a white coat, and a white hat, white shoes, the only thing missing was a falcon. Terrible. Like a giant panda with dropsy. She's that big, my mother-in-law, she stands in the garden in a vest, she looks like a wall of Snowcem. She hung her brassiere on the line to dry the other week and a camel was trying to make love to it. Well, she finished up fast asleep in our chair, she'd got her teeth out in a pile on the floor, mouth wide open, fast asleep. This mouse came out, jumped straight down her throat. I said to the wife, I'll fetch a piece of cheese and we'll waft it in front. I came back, the wife was wafting her with a piece of halibut. I said, that's not going to fetch a mouse out. Hang on, she said, I've got to get the bloody cat out first. Honest. Her mouth's that big. I remember once, she went swimming off Land's End. Almost drowned. It took three fellas to get her mouth open and give her the kiss of life. Two of them fell in, but the third one was saved. He was wearing skis. No, she's a sight, my mother-in-law. I remember once, she undressed without drawing the bedroom curtains and a Peeping Tom across the street gave himself up. Will that do?

All my in-laws are like that. Certainly. When they come for Christmas, it's like opening the door to a shoal of piranha fish. When they gathered round the mince pies, we had to get Eddie Waring in to do the commentary. Ta.

Eric Morecambe

You what? Well, yes, my favourite mother-in-law joke. There's the one about this man, this man, goes round to his next-door neighbours, says "Excuse me. Do you realise that your dog bit my mother-in-law this afternoon?" Fella says, "Oh. Terribly sorry about that I suppose you'll be suing me for damages, then?" Man says, "No. Not at all. How much will you take for the dog?" Weh-heh!

Ernie Wise

Do you know, before we were married, me and my wife that is, she said to me: "We really ought to buy a house close to mother's so that she can drop in whenever she's passing." Got this lovely house. Right on the banks of a river.

Dick Emery

My mother-in-law said to me, "When you die, I will dance on your grave. So I had it put in my will that I wanted to be buried at sea." Is that all right? Ooh, you are *awful*. But I like you.

Ken Dodd

Hello, young man. Well, your request has been fed into the Comical Computer at the Knotty Ash University, Department of Tickleology, and it has come up with the following definition of a mother-in-law, circa 1942, which is a

'Mother! Stop prying!'

military policeman in bloomers. Thank-you, thank-you. Another one I like: "I've bought my mother-in-law a Jaguar for Christmas. Marvellous. Tore her to pieces." One for the military men, "My mother-in-law, she was so fat, when we walked over a bridge, she had to break step." "My mother-in-law. Ugly? If Moses had seen her face first, there'd have been another Commandment. She had a face as though somebody had been chopping wood on it."

Bob Monkhouse

The thing about . my mother-in-law, she's sneaky. For example, she walks around without a bell round her neck. My wife once said to me, "what would convince you that her heart was in the right place?" I said, "an autopsy." No, in fact, I go up to Manchester regularly to see my mother-in-law. She lives in Newcastle, but she looks better seen from Manchester. Funny thing, my wife's mother didn't want me to marry her. You never know who your friends are until it's too late. I heard the other day that the Natural History Museum had found one of her old shoes. From it, they managed to reconstruct a Tyrannosaurus Rex. She's vicious. So vicious, that when lightning struck her once, it was in self-defence. Still, she's not spoken to me for three weeks. Not since I papered her room with travel posters.

Arthur Askey

Hello, there. You know, I was talking to this fella, he'd had a pretty bad time with his mother-in-law, a bit of an old hag, and eventually she died, of lock-jaw, and he went to the funeral, dutifully, trying to keep the smile off his face, and they were coming out of the church, there was a bit of a wind blowing, and this slate slid off the roof. Missed him by about half an inch. He looked up and he said, "Hello, You're up there already, are you?"

Ted Ray

My wife said to me, "My mother's coming over for Christmas."
I said, "Where's the dog?"
My wife said to me, "What's that got to do with it?"
I said, "Because I'm taking it to the vet."
She said, "Whatever for?"
I said, "To have his tail docked. I'm not having anyone in this house showing any sign of enjoying her visit."

Ken Goodwin

There was this fella once, he hated his mother-in-law that much, he got up an hour earlier each day to hate her that much longer. True. His mother-in-law was a lion-tamer. She didn't put her head in the lion's mouth, though. She'd got the lion putting its head in hers.

166

INTERVIEW:

AINSLEY GOTTO

talks to DAVID TAYLOR

LIKE the girl who dis-
covered Smirnoff, Miss
Ainsley Gotto had a routine
job in the typing-pool until
she tasted politics. She worked
her way up, joined the office
of the Prime Minister of
Australia (a bit of a lad, by
reputation*) and one witty,
bitch rejoinder brought her
a catty kind of charisma,
overnight. It's three years ago now, she was only twenty-
three but despite that—perhaps because of it—there had
already been some muttering suggestive of an up-coming
eminence grise, and a pretty one at that. Then came that
rejoinder. Erwin, a key minister in the John Gorton government, got the push; the result, he declared, of some "political
manoeuvre". What *kind* of political manoeuvre all of the
quick-on-the-uptake, lip-licking pressmen wanted to know.
"It's shapely, it wiggles, and its name is Ainsley Gotto."
And it was, and it did, and it was the name of the PM's
private secretary. "A piece of nonsense," she insists, but the
titters and the nudges had really begun.

The way that Ainsley Gotto stepped into the bar of a Park
Lane Hotel last Tuesday evening and ordered her own kind
of vodka highball, with ice, but no olive, I can well imagine
that they might. It isn't that she's flashy, not the *femme
fatale* sort to look at either, it's that she simply has class; and
aplomb; and a quick-witted look about her; and a wiggle.
She really can't help that wiggle (she was trained for some
years as a dancer) any more than she can help the smoky,
sloe-eyed good looks, the trim outline, the dress-sense. Only
just don't go on to assume that with all of that going for
her, Ainsley Gotto in any way used it; don't begin to suggest
either that John Gorton's obvious respect for Ainsley Gotto's
political acumen could conceivably have been blurred by his
taste for decorative things. She gets furious. As well she might.

For one thing, as she's quick to point out, once the

*"To get together with the boys and girls and relax a bit . . . is great . . . I
like a few drinks when I'm finished work. I like a party where I can sing and
dance and yarn."—Gorton, interviewed in *Age*, 1968.

rumours have begun to fly around it really isn't all that difficult to read things into the label of Private Secretary. Fleet Street proved her point at the time. It does *not* mean sitting around in jumpers going tippy-tap at the typewriter in between smiles. She told me so. Her job, as she described it, was an "administrative function" and pretty demanding at that. She got to it by way of the Economics Office and that of Australia's Chief Whip, and it was one of maintaining efficiency and liaison, as well as the (controversial) sifting of callers and the mail. "What was really super," she bubbled by way of example, "was to deal directly with the sort of people who wrote in to the PM's office because all else had failed, maybe someone who was going to get evicted, where the man had broken his leg at work and was still waiting for his compensation, where the woman had six kids to look after and couldn't get out to work, and where you felt you could really get something done to help them." She made it sound a little like the *Action Line* desk but I didn't press the point. We were convinced that the work was tough.

Miss Gotto is, too. Not one to let scandalmongering bother her—"It was really a piece of nonsense, untrue, and very unpleasant. You just don't have to let it swamp you, you have to shrug it off and get on with the job."—She wasn't broken either on other nasty occasions when her car

"I'm not quite sure how to put this darling, but ever since we've had the house modernised you don't fit in any more."

was slashed to ribbons or the morning post brought its regular sack of filth. That's politics. And she's out of it now, for good.

Ainsley Gotto left Gorton's office and Australia about a year after his defeat and took on executive assistance work with Canadian William Pollock, President of Drake International. She glows at the mention. "It's fabulous. It's a company that was basically built up by women and has grown to be the third largest of what I think you would loosely call the employment agency field." It sounded a bit too loose to me; it must, after all, be tricky to have reached the tops in career and publicity at the age of twenty-three and have nowhere to look but back down. Ainsley Gotto didn't agree. And after she'd given us a description of some of the places she's been flown around to lately and of her new apartment in Monte Carlo, I didn't agree either. She's still climbing.

"Please don't get the idea that I have expensive tastes," she said when we began to show signs. "But I do like beauty. With the world getting tougher and more miserable the whole time, I like my apartment to be a beautiful place and a peaceful one, nice paintings, nice furniture, that sort of thing. It hasn't happened yet, but that's the idea." She has this *terribly* pretty little laugh. She uses it now to punctuate random thoughts about how there are millions of dogs in Monte Carlo, about how the beach is all pebbly, not like Australia, which will always be home "even if one is realistic, as one tries to be, and one asks oneself what more there was to *do* there." This new job is so stimulating, too, she doesn't ever want to "stagnate". She has this cute way of smoking, the three spare fingers forming a decorative fan. What was she doing in London, by the way? "I'm here to have a look at the whole of the employment agency business in the UK." I do like a girl with freckles.

———————————

A lady of many hobbies, she makes woollen rabbits and, on the political front, she recently read a book by Enoch Powell.　　　　　　　　　　　　*(Bournemouth Echo)*

A woman on her way to Scarborough to see a probation officer got drunk and went on a fishing boat with an Eskimo to Iceland, the Borough Court heard today.
　　　　　　　　　　　　　　(Scarborough Evening News)

Doreen Irvin, a former prostitute known as "Darling Doreen", who claims to have been both a drug addict and a witch and to have taken part in the exhumation of bodies for the worship of Satan, gave a talk to Young Wives at Maulden Baptist Church this week.　　　*(Luton News)*

Are You Going To Believe Raquel Welch?

when you could be believing
STANLEY REYNOLDS?

TORMENT OF THE WORLD'S No. 1 SEX SYMBOL

RAQUEL: THE ULTIMATE WOMAN
"IT'S NO FUN BEING THE WORLD'S MOST BEAUTIFUL WOMAN."

Raquel Welch lay back on three pillows for support, looking pale, drawn but better without make-up. It was 12.30 p.m. in her villa in the South of France, where I interviewed her, and she had only just woken up . . . She wore a winceyette top that hugged her figure in the softest of caresses.

What kind of man turns Raquel on? "I like a man to be a man."

DAY after day, the other week, Mr. Terry O'Neill, with a little help from the Ultimate Woman herself, was proving that the era of stardust glitter journalese is alive and gasping for breath in the *Daily Express*.

Glamour and heartbreak, the heartbreak behind the tinsel of show biz, the broken heart for every light on the old marquee, was Mr. O'Neill's strong card on the Raquel caper. When she developed what she coyly referred to as "the equipment," men, she said, started treating her like "a piece of meat", pushing her in front of the movie camera, telling her when to sit down, when to stand up, and giving her nothing but the dross of wealth and the pottage of fame as compensation. If it weren't for her kids, the villa in France, the cars, the diamonds, and the numbered bank account in Zurich and points West, she'd have given up the ghost a long time ago.

But somehow, I couldn't seem to get over the slight suspicion that Mr. O'Neill had been led up the villa path down there on the Côte d'Azur. Let's face it, this kid Welch has not only starred in, but also produced, *Kansas City Bomber* which is steaming the box offices coast-to-coast all over Yankland right now. This kid Welch is not just a star, she is a business tycoon. Ever since the *Express* series there has been appearing before my eyes a sort of a dream, in which, of course, any resemblance to persons living or dead is strictly unintentional.

The scene is the Riviera villa bedroom of that billion-dollar property, Annunziata Muldoon, she of the flashing Spanish gypsy beauty and the laughing Irish eyes. At curtain, Annunziata has just polished off a pair of brunch kippers and is lighting up a mid-morning cigar, perusing the latest stock market results in the Wall Street Journal, Barrum's Weekly, *and the* Financial Times. *Telephones lie at the ready by each of her dimpled elbows. A worried frown knits her marbled brow.*

ANNUNZIATA: Up, up, up. All my stocks keep soaring. And this is supposed to be a recession. I gotta get me some kind of a nice tax loss but every lousy thing I touch turns to blue chip. *(Picking up a telephone.)* Gimme Schnell, Raus, and Himmel in New York. Hello, Harry? Oh, it's Moe. Listen, Moe, what's this crud about me not being able to buy Uraguay for cryin' out loud? I own it already, huh? Well, listen, Moe, don't just stand there. Sell it. And buy Paraguay. Half a guay is better than none. And get me a nice tax loss, will you? How come I gotta tell you guys everything for cryin' out loud?

(She replaces the receiver just as a man enters. This is Harvey Undergrowth, her new private secretary, a mild-mannered man in a chalk-stripe suit, tortoiseshell specs, his hair plastered back and neatly parted.)

ANNUNZIATA: Who the hell are you?

UNDERGROWTH: Undergrowth, Miss Muldoon. The new man.

ANNUNZIATA: Yeah, well stop creepin' up on me like that when you burst in on me. When you burst in on me, make some noise.

UNDERGROWTH: M-m-m-m . . .

ANNUNZIATA: Come on, man, spit it out. Spit it on the wall, for cryin' out loud, so I can read it. I ain't got all day, there's a delegation of Swiss bankers coming here this afternoon for a laying on of hands and I want to run through them figures on Anaconda Copper. And frankly, I went over the books on Mesopotopian Gulf Oil this a.m. and I think the readings on the original bore drillings is a whole bunch of crud, Undergrowth. If I can't suck twelve hundred barrels a day out of that place, why, at 7½ per cent repayments on the second mortgage, we won't be realising more than 5, 5½ on a deal like that. I'd just as soon teach my grandmother to suck eggs as go into a crud set-up like that. And stop standing there so quiet, Undergrowth. And, Undergrowth, stop fidgeting.

UNDERGROWTH: It's M-M-M Mister B-B-B Buck, y-y-y-y our p-p-p . . .

ANNUNZIATA: Yeh, yeh, Nimrod Buck, my press agent. They teach you to stutter like that at Harvard Business School,

Undergrowth? What you wanna do is stick some rocks in your mouth and go down and shout at the swimming pool. It works wonders. Listen, Undergrowth, I know this winceyette top is hugging this equipment of mine in the softest of caresses and it troubles you. But, cryin' out loud, it's torment for me. You work around here you gotta get used to seein' the most beautiful woman in the world.

(*Nimrod Buck, the press agent with the eyes of a pawn-broker and the smile of a barracuda, enters.*)

BUCK: For cryin' out loud, Nunzi, what ya doin' ta me? I got a feature writer from the *Daily Express* waitin' downstairs an' you ain't even half-dressed. Get half-dressed quick. (*To Under-growth*) Say, what the hell is this. Get them addin' machines the hell outta here, and clean up that ticker tape for cryin' out loud. (*To Annunziata who is getting back into bed*) Nunzi, baby, how could you? To me? What wuz you before I took over? Runnin' that lousy loft in Wall Street, sellin' a little stock here, cornerin' a little wheat there. Strictly a nickels and dimes outfit. You wuzn't even listed on the big board for cryin' out loud.

ANNUNZIATA (*arranging an outrageous décolletage*): What the hell's with this *Daily Express?* Why can't they profile my holding companies or something really innarestin' like that Tanzanian zinc merger for gosh sake's?

(*Enter the Expressman.*)

ANNUNZIATA (*pretending to be only waking*): What is the hour? Yawn, yawn, stretch, stretch.

EXPRESSMAN: Gone noon, Miss Muldoon. What's that top you're wearing made out of? Silk, huh? Or a sort of nylon? A sort of silky nylon you'd call it, I suppose? Boy, it clings to the equipment like the softest of I don't know what.

ANNUNZIATA: Gosh, noon already, and I been up filmin' onna location all night already and then chewin' my nails ha'f the night wunnerin' if it's worth all the heart break. If it wasn't fer them wunnerful kids a mine, Carlos and Sasha . . .

BUCK: Jake and Tom, for cryin' outloud, you dumb broad.

ANNUNZIATA: I wouldn't know what ta do with myself, honest ta God, fer Gawd's sake, I wouldn't, you know what I mean? It's called winceyette. Kind of hugs my figure sort of like the softest caresses don't it?

EXPRESSMAN (*writing*): W-i-n-c . . . Lots of heart break I'll bet in this sex symbol game, huh?

ANNUNZIATA: Oh, you betcha. Heart break ain't in it. It's more like torment, know what I mean? Say, you speak real good fer a ferriner.

EXPRESSMAN: Tell me, Miss Muldoon, what kind of man turns you on?

ANNUNZIATA: Well, right now I'm looking for an accountant who can cost a job right on the spot, no messing . . .

BUCK: Nix, nox, you dumb bimbo. (*To the reporter.*) Nunzi likes a guy to be . . . ah . . . a guy, like, don't you, honey?

ANNUNZIATA: Yeah, that's right. Speakin' frankly I like a man to be a man.

EXPRESSMAN: How do you spell winceyette?

BUCK: An' the loneliness of bein' a top-flight sex symbol for all the chumps. That really bothers her. Don't it, babe?

ANNUNZIATA: I'll say. Yeh, loneliness ain't in it. It's more a kind of a torment. W-i-n-c-e— Hey, Undergrowth, how you spell winceyette? I got wealth and fame, diamonds and poils, three bootiful kiddies . . .

BUCK: Two, two bootiful kiddies. It's two. W-i-n-c—

EXPRESSMAN: Is that E, double T-E, or just one T?

ANNUNZIATA: But what does the world know of a lonely woman's heart behind all the tinsel? Two bummer marriages. An accountant who don't know double entry book-keepin' from a hole in the ground, and not a real good tax dodge in sight. Torment ain't even in the runnin'.

EXPRESSMAN: Maybe I ought to just make it "silky fabric". What do you think, Miss Muldoon?

ANNUNZIATA: I think there's a broken heart for every light on the marquee. Two E's.

EXPRESSMAN (rising): Thank you, Miss Muldoon.

ANNUNZIATA: Don't mention it, I'm sure.

(Exit the Expressman in search of a dictionary.)

ANNUNZIATA (to Undergrowth): Come on, get the lead out. I got the United Artist bankers skying in from New York tonight. Get me Kubrick on the phone. Sell my zinc, buy copper, and ask Steve McQueen what the hell he means holding out for ten per cent of the gross, who the hell does he think he is, Raquel Welch already? And by the by, call London, and buy the Daily Express; I think we might have a nice tax loss there.

(During this speech Annunziata dresses in a plain, charcoal business suit, ties up her hair, puts on horn rimmed glasses. Nimrod Buck leaves in disgust, but the hitherto timid Harvey Undergrowth seems mesmerised. He walks towards her as if he were in a dream, as if he were seeing her for the first time).

UNDERGOWTH (lovingly): Why, mm M-M-M- Miss M-M-Muldoon you . . . y-y-y-you're . . . e-e-e-e f-f-ficient.

(Together they sit side by side poring over Anaconda copper while the adding machine plays.)

CURTAIN

Bristol girl Vivian Rice (23) has signed her own peace treaty with the Indians—by marrying a member of the Flathead tribe in America. She is now Mrs. Vivian Rice Red Wing Nine Pipe, wife to Louie Nine Pipe, whose age is estimated at between 74 and 84 years. "It's rather a fairy tale, don't you think?" Mrs. Nine Pipe said today.

(Bristol Evening Post)

Women &
Beauty

FRASCINO

"Is my face straight?"

"He's simply divine, I had to slap him last time."

"It's your husband, Mrs. Sanborn, are you here?"

"... and not a minute too soon ..."

"Now don't talk me into anything that will make my husband angry, you naughty boy."

"Can you step in here a moment, Mr. Paul? I'd like a second opinion."

"All right, Margaret, I know you're in here some place!"

To See a Fine Lady Ride on a White Horse

ANN LESLIE talks to a people's hero

LITTLE pink effigies of Mr. Heath fashioned in coconut-ice; his portrait twinkling in fairylights over the boiled sweets in the nation's corner shop; his piano-key teeth picked out in municipal marigolds from Potter's Bar to Tenby. . . . And airline posters everywhere proclaiming "One Nation! One Leader! One Ted!"

Alas, such heady hero-worship is likely to remain but a mad dream as far as British Prime Ministers are concerned. But in India things are different and right now Mrs. Indira Gandhi is getting the above works in full. Air India posters carry the slogan "One Nation! One Leader! One Indira!" in letters three feet high. As a massive electoral vote of thanks to the lady for having punched Bhutto on the nose, the Indians have slung her political rivals into the wilderness and are busily tacking up her image on mango trees and mud huts and the walls of every steaming, cow-littered slum in the land.

Naturally, the infatuation isn't universal, and some sections of Indian society have good cause to feel a bit cheesed off about the whole Indira affair. Maharajas, for a start. Having had their privy purses whisked away, they're reduced to flogging off the ancestral rubies, putting the elephants out to grass and wrapping cellophane bandages round the palace loos to reassure hygiene-mad American tourists that all has now been "Sanitized for Your Convenience".

Moreover, nepotism being a flourishing cottage industry in Indian politics, scores of deposed M.P.s are lurking glumly in their air-conditioned bungalows, sipping black-market chota pegs and wondering what on earth to do with all those uncles, brothers, sons and fourth-cousins-twice-removed whose chappatties have thus been rudely snatched from their indolent mouths by an ungrateful electorate.

Indira, they muttered, is a Red in tooth and claw and no good will come to the spirit of Indian free enterprise if she tries to deprive the bourgeoisie of their time-honoured opportunities for making a dishonest crust. And I can't imagine that the scribbling army of Indian civil servants—who've turned Delhi's imperial garden city into a series of monumental red sandstone filing cabinets—can be feeling too secure since Mrs. Gandhi was heard to describe their promotion system as "dead wood replacing dead wood".

But then you can't please everyone. Running a democracy has always been a pretty thankless task, what with all those back-seat drivers shouting and waving their arms and telling you you've lost your way. Indira Gandhi, in charge of the world's largest democracy, has over 500 million back-seat drivers, speaking fourteen different languages, 250 different dialects, all trying to instruct her on how to steer the great ramshackle machine along a road pot-holed with the most terrifying social and economic problems on earth.

But if all that power and all those problems appal her, she's not the sort of cosy old duck who'd let on about it. "I'm too busy to be frightened," she told me recently as we sat talking in her cavernous, wood-panelled office in New Delhi. The room, once used by her father, Nehru, has the cheerless dignity of a funeral parlour with few personal touches to relieve its reverential gloom.

There's a picture of a horse. A bronze of Nataraja, the god of dance, "not a very good one, I'm afraid". Some yellow roses.

Mrs. Gandhi sits behind a monumental desk, a handsome, aloof woman of grave and wintry charm, whose noble Nehru nose, once fractured by a flying brick, lends her the air of a patrician hawk. As she talks, she plays with a pencil. Courtiers scuttle in and out like mice for whispered consultations. A photographer buzzes to and fro, and, for a moment, ripples of irritation cross her impassive face. "No, I don't like having my picture taken. But there are lots of things about this job I don't like." Such as? "Oh, having to live in this dreadful heat. I never really wanted to go into politics: I just wanted to go and live in a cold climate!" Outside, the ground is shimmering like a beaten gong under hammer-blows of white sun. She looks distant, murmuring: "Mountains . . . mountains, they are my great love."

The Nehru family, aristocratic Brahmins, came from the Himalayan border state of Kashmir. It is there that Mrs. Gandhi spent her honeymoon, there she scattered her father's ashes.

Once imprisoned by the British for political agitation, she christened her cell after the mountain Chimborazo. "For some reason at school I was always terribly bored with geography but the names of the Latin-American peaks have always enchanted me. Besides, I've always loved that poem— 'Romance', I think it's called—do you know it?" She begins to recite it: " 'Chimborazo! Cotapaxi! They have stolen my soul away!' . . ."

"Another difficulty I have experienced in my chosen way of life is that I am very shy. Oh yes I am. I've just learnt how to hide it better over the years."

"When my father first asked me to act as his official hostess I was terrified. At first I said, okay, I'll make all the arrangements but when the guests come, I won't come down. It wasn't that I didn't like crowds. I've always been used to crowds, helping my father at political meetings and such like. But I'd always been surrounded by people at home, writers, painters, politicians, who were passionately involved in *something*. It was the thought of making small talk about nothing that scared me to death . . ."

"What have I had to give up for my job? Exercise. I miss that terribly. I am getting dreadfully depressed, you know, about my weight, sitting in offices all day." She was once a keen skier. "I even started a winter sports club here near Simla but I've never had enough time to go there more than twice." Instead, she starts every day at five o'clock in the morning with a set of yoga exercises.

A passion for exercise is hardly typical of upper-middle-class Indian ladies, whose idea of suitable leisure activities usually seems to involve little more than lolling happily about like big brown seals, guzzling sweetmeats and gossiping with their female relations. But then Mrs. Gandhi hardly resembles that archetype of Indian womanhood, the creature who glides about in the shadow of her menfolk, oozing femininity and humble subservience to the male ego. Mrs. Gandhi is an altogether tougher cookie: "I've never been in the shadow of anybody, not even my father. I've always been very determined and very independent."

The fact that a nation of male chauvinists like India can happily vote a woman into power is just another of those dotty paradoxes in which this baffling and schizophrenic people revel. Mrs. Gandhi doesn't find anything odd about it at all and quite clearly finds the whole subject of being a woman Prime Minister too boring to discuss. "I do not regard myself as a woman but a person with a job to do."

If, as some feel, she is arrogant, even snobbish, it's hardly surprising. The heir to the royal family of Indian politics (her only brother died within three days of his birth), she's always been in the public eye: "Even as a student in England I was treated as if I were somebody and in India I have been somebody all my life."

Her marriage to a Parsi newspaperman and politician, Feroze Gandhi (no relation to the Mahatma), was not, she admits, "ideally happy" since her husband understandably disliked being referred to as "the nation's son-in-law". As his wife remarked, "He would get upset, and it would take me weeks to win him over. To hurt the male ego is, of course, the biggest sin in marriage."

Feroze Gandhi died twelve years ago. Mrs. Gandhi is now a grandmother, her two sons are engineers and neither intend going into politics. "I've never wanted them to."

I asked her if she ever felt lonely: "Loneliness is largely a state of mind and doesn't depend on how many people surround you. I don't have that lonely state of mind. But . . ." she played with the pencil for a while ". . . there's no doubt about it, once you reach the top, in whatever sphere of life, you are always bound to feel a little . . . separate. If that is loneliness, well . . ."

179

RIGHT BETWEEN THE EYES

BASIL BOOTHROYD
noses out a sensational new trend

NO name dropper, I refer all the same to my friend Fanny Cradock, whose husband taught me how to open champagne without that vulgar pop, which is neither here nor there, now I come to think of it. Nor is the fact that if our association is now on a mere Christmas card basis, that's because I never had the nerve to return her hospitality, and she must lose lots of friends that way.

It was about nineteen years ago that Fanny picked her new —let's put that another way. When she chose her new nose in collaboration with Sir Archibald MacIndoe* some nineteen years ago, she did it by leafing through a stack of French glossies and superimposing a selection of pleasing conks on photographs of her own. This was typically practical. A nose by any other shape may smell as sweet, but set it in an alien landscape and it may be a stinker. A Bardot, for instance, or a Margaret Thatcher, desirable enough in itself, may prove after the unveiling ceremony to clash hopelessly with its new ears. Shift the ears a centimetre, with a bit of lobe-trimming if necessary, and your cheekbones don't fit. You could end up with the whole site redeveloped, and people asking your husband who was that lady they saw him with last night.

A lot of women don't realise this, if I'm to believe Dr. Hans G. Bruck of Vienna, who appears in these pages fresh from a meeting of brother scalpels in Miami. His subject was the changing trends in feminine nose fashions, and since he's re-hootered over five thousand distraught lady patients, during a long career with the healing knife, his views aren't to be sniffed at. Indeed, the *Herald Tribune,* scenting a story (I'm afraid you're in for a lot of this kind of thing, but I'll try to fight it), jetted their rhino-plastery correspondent into sunny Florida whence he telexed the paper as follows:

"Dr. Bruck said that whereas women used to come into his office clutching pictures of Mrs. Jackie Onassis, they now thrust photos of Princess Anne into his hands."

This dramatic switch from American to British Royalty at the top of the nose charts will swell many a home and Commonwealth heart. The ladies of Boston may look down their—may not, that is, be too happy, but there you are: fashion is a volatile tyrant, and you're bound to get these fluctuations. I don't know how long the ex-White House

*Her book, *Something's Burning*, Putnam, 1960

prototype was being shoved under Dr. Bruck's—I'll rephrase that; just how long Jackie's snub little snoot led the field, I don't know, and a glance through the casebook would be interesting, if only to throw light, as kindly as possible, on preceding champions. Earlier patients probably had their crushes on Mesdames Eva Peron and Chiang Kai-Shek, with the occasional welcome variant, say, of Mrs. Khrushchev, Golda Meir or Marlene Dietrich . . . and there's a nose, incidentally, I'd be proud to blow.

What seems certain is that no sufferers ever rushed in clutching pictures of an unknown nose from Willesden, Cincinatti or Adelaide. Your run-of-the-mill housewife in Edgbaston or Zurich, even with a nose that would make Cleopatra's seem like a rock cake, can't hope for a look-in. These noses have to be prominent, let's change that to eminent, or their therapeutic properties are nil. Get your new nose out of the better gossip columns or nowhere, is the guiding rule. And, even so, prepare yourself for its lapse from grace. It can be hell when the nose you've selected for its star quality, and flashed around your friends, full face and profile,

"Before I unload, I wonder if I might have an estimate?"

until they begin to think it should have a CRO number stamped across it, suddenly drops out of the Social Register. Where does an ex-celebrity's nose rank as a conversation piece? Worse, the original proprietor may herself decide on a replacement, and it's hard to say which is more of an incubus, an ex-celebrity's nose, or a celebrity's ex-nose. Oh, no, you need the Cradock pragmatism to love a nose for its own sake, filched from no more distinguished a source than an anonymous brunette modelling suedes in *Paris Match*.

What, you may wonder, will be Princess Anne's reaction to this latest accolade? Did she know that her nose was tipped, you might say, for the transplant stakes? Being at present in South East Asia—where the general run of noses (damn), though well designed for local flute playing, fails of widespread appeal in the west, her feelings are hard to come at. Rest assured, however, that a palace spokesman will have been left behind in SW1 to make what statements he can, and he will, I know, respond helpfully to telephoned enquiries about Princess Anne's nose. Your call may have to seep through a switchboard already log-jammed by accredited court correspondents and their eager if predictable questions: How does the Princess feel about her new distinction? Is she pleased that it went to her, instead of Mrs. Tricia Cox, née Nixon? Will she be embarrassed, or what, if her nose gets to be so popular that all the women at her next Royal Premier receiving line are wearing it? Does she plan to give up show-jumping, in case she falls on it, ruins it, and drops clean out of the charts in favour of Eartha Kitt? Has she any intention of changing her own nose, thus playing the very devil with good old Doc Hans's mugshot book? And so on. Well, perhaps you'll get bored with the unobtainable signal in the end, and hang up.

If so, perhaps I can help you a bit. Still no name-dropper, except in a context of utter relevance, I can say, and with relish, that I have had breakfast with Princess Anne's nose. We didn't discuss it, and I'm not sure that it's very gentlemanly to mention relish just there like that, but your trained observer is a prisoner of his natural instincts. We weren't alone. The Bishop of Bath and Wells was there, and we didn't discuss his (sometimes called the parson's) nose, either. I can report, then, that the Princess's nose, as now being worn in Vienna, is a good nose as noses go. Lacking a micrometer I could only guess at its length, which is about right, with just the needed degree of concavity to prevent fun sunglasses, even if they get bigger this summer, from slipping off into the barbecued roast. Firm, adequately fleshed at the bridge—where your lesser nose can often exhibit tautness and mottling—I would sum it up as a nose which Her Royal Highness would be wise to hang on to, even in the face of future trends towards that of, say, Mrs. Indira Gandhi, Twiggy, or Baroness Wootton.

If I add, in all honesty, that my opinion of it resembles that of Dr. Samuel G. Johnson on the Giant's Causeway: namely, that while it is a nose worth seeing, it is not a nose worth going to see, then I am confident that its owner would say the same, and if she formed a similar view, if any, of mine, it's probable that the absence of any intended disrespect is mutual.

And, talking of mine, because we all come back to ourselves in the end, even with other people's noses, I'm wondering if the new noses for men kick, at present restricted to fugitives from justice, will hit us while I'm still young enough to take advantage of it.

I'm thinking, I may say, more as a giver than a receiver. It's simply that this seems a good time to give notice, before the rush starts, that my nose, as soon as I can get my lawyer and agent out to lunch, is going to be copyright. So put that in your hankie and wipe it.

"Gerald! There's something growing in the garden again!"

"Don't knock your wife about: it doesn't do any good." Mr. Justice Faulks
True or False?

The PUNCH Think-Tank holds a hearing.

Witness A. *(Male, 63, Mole-poacher)*

"It's like most things in the world, sometimes it does and sometimes it doesn't, like. I've had four o' them myself. Numbers one and three responded to a bashing, number two turned mulish, number four bashed back. It's always worth trying, that's my advice."

Witness B. *(Male, 28, hors d'oeuvres Nutritionist)*

"It's a very unscientific remark. What is the size of the sample? What is the size of the control-group? Does the term 'knock about' extend to Grievous Bodily Harm? How does the judge know, not guess, know, that, in the cases on which he bases his opinion, the treatment was not broken off too soon?"

Witness C. *(Male, 9, Chorister)*

"I meant to bash my wife when I grew up; but, if it's a waste of time, I won't. Grownups are good at knowing when to take things easy. And judges are about as grownup as grownups can get. I played a trick on my girlfriend. I made

"The fact he couldn't look you in the eyes is hardly evidence, Mrs. Bronson."

her sit in some jam and then took her for a walk past a wasps nest."

Witness D. *(Female, mid-twenties, Bishop's Secretary)*

"All women should be trained in karate. No man whose spouse can crumble a breezeblock with a backhander is going to try to mould her the hard way. Wives should also be well trained in judo and Cornish wrestling; even a man she has met on the mat is unlikely to know the counterholds for Old Tyme Falls. Women should be armed in the home, not merely with the usual cosh and skewer, but with such firearms as . . . Oh, is my time up?"

Witness E. *(Male, 37, cabaret act—The Demon Dentist)*

"All the judge, or any judge, can say is that bashing doesn't make a wife better. He can't know that not bashing one doesn't allow her to become worse. There's a lot of deterioration among women and some of it could well be due to never having a hand lifted against them."

Witness F. *(Female, 17, Underground Theatre Usherette)*

"The judge didn't say it was no use for a woman to beat up a man. I thought it was rather marked, the way he omitted the point. My friend Délice has a boy who won't go home with her without wearing a skidlid, she's so handy with the knuckles. I bet Délice would be a good influence on that judge."

Witness G. *(Female, late-forties, ex-Duchess)*

"My worst fault is that I'm a soup-thrower. Three husbands have tried to cure me by blows. All have failed."

Witness H. *(Male, 83, retired Midshipman)*

"It may not do any good. That doesn't mean it's not worth doing. When I was a lad—and we lived hard and clean in those days—you weren't always asking, 'Am I going to get any advantage out of doing this?' A man did what a man had to do. People laugh when you tell them that in the long ago the world was a less materialistic place. But it is sober truth. Women, like children, dogs, Africans and recruits, must be treated with firmness; man owes it to his place in Nature. A king must reign."

Witness I. *(Female, 66, Wardress)*

"I simply don't think that men are any good at knocking women about."

Conclusion

This thought-provoking judicial comment is (a) Thought-provoking (b) Unconvincing (c) Makes one want to know more about Mr. Justice Faulks.

You Called Me Baby Doll a Year Ago...

claims SALLY VINCENT

BEFORE I embarked upon the inward journey by way of paper-back dream analyses, five-guineas-an-hour psychiatrists and R. D. Laing, I was free, as it were, to travel abroad in innocence. I imagined, in my simple way, that possession of passport, ticket and currency entitled me to the ambition of slopping around Mediterranean beaches inducing my body to go all toffee-coloured and my mind to broaden, gently as menopausal hips, to such information as Proust, Stendhal or Tolstoy have to offer.

Innocence, like ignorance, is nothing if not pretentious. Fortunately (or not as the case might be) it doesn't last; reality is constantly indecently exposing itself to those of us with impeccable motives and forcing our blameless eyes to gaze upon its monstrous face. I might *think* I'm a girl whose intentions are limited to sunbathing away an acne crop while taking in a novel, but what protection can my naive processes achieve against the fact that everyone else knows differently. She who sallies forth upon an inhabited beach is exhibiting herself for the sexual approval of males who believe, along with the mosquitoes, that her body is free. She is a willing rapee with no right even to select the identity of the rapist.

Sexual approach in these sunny circumstances is irrevocably entwined with sexual hostility, as I learned to the cost of twenty-seven and six when I was about seventeen. I was crouched harmlessly over the Dud Avocado on the banks of the Seine when one of those Algerian fellows with no forehead and gold teeth in the front elected to sit up against me as though there was an overcrowding problem and bad-breathed at me something approximating a deep and life-long alliance for the pair of us, commencing with a walk in the direction of his choice. Since my French was then fairly

"Do you realise that's our last virgin."

unequivocal I was able to enunciate clearly that I wished to be alone to read my book, thank-you and goodbye. But it wasn't until I had repreated my kindly phrases about nine times that I realized he had painstakingly burned a huge hole in my skirt with his Gauloise.

In the years following this initiation I learned to defend myself with less linguistics. I can say "I do not speak" in eight languages and I'm working on a ninth. Unfortunately this method is not always successfully repelling. I remember, particularly, an ugly scene on the beach at Malaga, when I was beaten about the head and shoulders with a superman comic by a young Spaniard in a frenzy of frustration because to his fuddled little brain "no ablar Espagnol" meant precisely the reverse. If you know three words, he reasoned beneath his black hair and religious medallions, you know them all. Which, strange as it migh seem, is a sentiment not uncommon among beach boys. Many of them go to the strain of equipping themselves with a formidable list of three-worders, so that when "are—you—Engleesh?" hits the spot they reckon themselves half way to your hotel bedroom. Hell hath no fury like a beach boy when you tell them you're waiting for a friend and some have extended their vocabulary to include such exit lines as "you are fat," "you are thin," "you are mean" and "you are old."

I must, however, confess that even in the midst of such habitual and squalid encounters, I still believe romance is to be found on foreign soil.

Indeed, once upon a time and very far away in a place I shall call, for the sake of respectable anonymity, Greece, I fell madly in love with a correctly introduced and splendidly handsome young man. I knew from the way he clicked his heels together and made a little bow from the neck that he was a serious person. Our relationship, to put it mildly, blossomed, wonderfully assisted as it was by the fact that his English was none too brilliant We were, therefore, unable to indulge ourselves in the sort of disillusioning communication occasioned by the sophistry of a mutual tongue. Romance, as everyone knows, thrives on little mysteries like not knowing the first thing about each other. Three weeks passed in a kind of light-headed paradise, stabilized only by my absolute certainty that I had met Mr. Right and there remained only a few details such as immigration, marriage and repatriation between me and happy-ever-after. I was, of course, peacefully discouraged from checking the efficacy of my dreams against the broken English of any kind of a response.

One day, in the full flood of my passion, I found myself alone in his apartment while he was out buying me yet another token of his esteem. Time was feather-light in my hands as I revelled in the presence of the possessions of the loved-one, engrossed in that frenetic awareness of things where an object, such as a collar stiffener, takes on a beautiful significance that has previously, in one's other blindly love-less state, been elusive. My absorption in the trinkets of his daily life gradually developed, not to put too fine a point on it, into a desire to snoop. Drawers and cupboards became open drawers and cupboards and busy little fingers were rapidly rifling their contents.

The prize find was a parcel of letters which I shamelessly made available to myself, sorting the English from the foreign and gobbling up their messages in hysterical haste lest the door open and my fervent dedication mistaken for an obscene disrespect for privacy.

They were, as luck would have it, all love-letters. Love-letters, indeed, of a singular quality, somewhat banal in style and high-pitched in tone. "My pillow is wet with tears because you are no longer in my arms," was the kind of thing. And "sweet pussycat I long for a glimpse of your beauty." It was compulsive, even hot stuff, but there was something intangibly *odd* about them all that I could not explain to myself as mere lack of literacy. It was not until I had snaffled up the tenth—"will I ever forget the joy of your embrace"—that a signature caught my eye. "Robert," it said. Quite distinctly. I checked through the pack. "John," they had written, "Martin," "Claude," "Richard." There was no question about it, I was the only woman in his life. Which might have been some comfort to me on the flight home. No, one will never again travel innocently. But hopefully is always another matter.

"He never watches at home."

Dock Briefs

FENTON BRESLER looks at lust and the law

I DON'T know why Tennyson wrote that it was only young men's fancy that lightly turns in the Spring to thoughts of love. There is no age limit on that particular pastime. And it does not only happen in the Spring.

Legally, there is no harm in giving way to thoughts of pleasant dalliance provided both parties agree; they are of age; and display a proper sense of time and place. It's not so much what you do, but when—and where—you choose to do it.

The first prerequisite is to make sure that you've got the right partner. Cambridge magistrates did not give a very sympathetic hearing to the 22-year-old member of a pop group who, when pleading guilty recently to indecently assaulting a girl on a bus, explained that he was on a LSD "trip" and thought the girl, a perfect stranger, was his wife. They fined him £30—which, for a first offence and a comparatively minor indecency, is quite steep nowadays.

The second rule, of course, is to ensure that the young lady is truly a consenting party. It must be a freely given consent, unsullied by fraud or anything more dishonest than the usual male lies. All may well be fair in love and war, but legally there is a limit.

One should never go so far as the smooth-talking Irish labourer who, last summer, convinced a singularly gullible young London barmaid that he was a doctor and then persuaded her to strip naked for an examination. The poor girl was only suffering from a sore throat, and the Marylebone stipendiary magistrate gave the fellow a three-months' gaol sentence. Personally, I'd have thought he deserved a letter of recommendation to Henry Kissinger: a man like that would be an asset to any able negotiator's staff.

I must admit I've always had a special affection for the game of "doctor and patient" ever since I used to play it at the age of eight with a girl called Pamela. Mind you, even then, I was conscious of the need to choose carefully one's time and place: my consulting room was always the garage at the bottom of our garden and visiting hours were always when Dennis, the gardener-cum-chauffeur, was out driving my father.

For the over-riding legal principle is that kissing and cuddling—and more—is for private premises; not for public places.

Indeed, it is remarkable how sternly the law regards public manifestation of private passion. When a few years ago, Dr. Billy Graham expressed his surprise and disapproval at the recumbent, embracing couples in London's parks, he was only echoing the words of most Park Regulations throughout the country which list as "prohibited acts": "Behaving or being clothed in any manner reasonably likely to offend against public decency."

The shocked evangelist would have been legally entitled to have called a policeman and have had the whole lot arrested.

"Public indecency" is an offence against various Acts of Parliament, innumerable local by-laws—and ancient Common Law. Mr. Ross McWhirter and Mrs. Mary Whitehouse would no doubt be delighted to know that the courts have accepted the dictionary definition of "indecency" as "that which is unbecoming or immodest", which certainly includes a public kiss—except possibly kissing an elderly relative goodbye at a railway station.

In fact, it is frightfully difficult for a fellow to kiss a girl in public without incurring severe legal displeasure. The great British out-of-doors is sacrosanct. Young lovers might think

"Have you any idea how long it's been since you last bit me on the ear?"

that a quiet spot in the rough on some remote golf course might perhaps be a suitable place to pass the time of day. But they will usually be breaking the law.

Club links are private property and 'strangers' only legal right, at best, is to "pass and re-pass". Once they lie down or merely stop and look deep into each other's eyes, they become trespassers and can be asked to leave.

If they stand and embrace in the street, they are liable to have a policeman ask them to move along. They are causing an obstruction of the footway. Pavements—like golf courses —are to be used only for "passing and re-passing": a stationary kiss becomes a statutory offence.

If the couple think they will be cunning and stand by a bus stop as if waiting for a bus, they will still be breaking the law. For the Public Service Vehicles (Conduct of Drivers, Conductors and Passengers) Regulations of 1936 clearly state: "Passengers and intending passengers shall not conduct themselves in a riotous or disorderly manner". I'm not sure exactly how far one has to go to be "riotous", but last summer a young man, responding to the romantic impulses of life in Stoke-on-Trent, was fined £3 by the local magistrates' court for "conducting himself in a disorderly manner" in trying to kiss the girl sitting next to him on a bus.

Although some of my more pleasant teenage memories relate to visits to the cinema without particular reference to what was being shown on the screen, I must confess that my back-row activities could have lost those various houses of entertainment their licence. Necking in the dark while glamorous figures flitter across the silver screen may be pleasurable, but it is technically unlawful. If a cinema manager tolerates it, he is liable to lose his licence, for one of the many conditions which local Councils impose on picture houses is: "No impropriety of dance or gesture or anything which is in any way offensive to public feeling shall be permitted on the premises". Strange, really, when I recall that the most successful of the small cinemas in Brighton where, as they say, I spent my formative years, was a little "flea-pit"—now, alas, closed down—where the thoughtful management provided double seats in their back rows with no dividing arm-rest.

Railway by-laws forbid canoodling in trains, local by-laws frequently penalise it in parked motor cars on the road, the Ecclesiastical Courts Jurisdiction Act of 1860 says it shall not be done in the churchyard of any Church of England church or chapel. Even "committing a nuisance in a telephone kiosk" is a specific crime against the Post Office Act of 1953. If the law were fully enforced, love-making in this country would be a virtual impossibility—except for those fortunate actors and actresses who perform on our television screens.

But perhaps the most startling limitation on the Briton's freedom to "do his own thing" occurred last December, when Norwich magistrates had a rather unusual case before them.

A 39-year-old local instrument maker didn't just look upon his back lawn as a place to have tea. For him and his 33-year-old wife, it was a place to make love.

Unfortunately, there was no fence or thick hedge dividing their bungalow's garden from their neighbour's: merely, a row of flowers. Two young children in the next-door garden spotted them through the flowers—and told their mother. She called in the police.

The husband and wife were duly charged. Their offence? He was accused of indecent exposure in his own back garden, and she with aiding and abetting. They both pleaded Not Guilty. "I love my wife and I cannot see why we should not show some affection to each other," said the man.

But the Norwich magistrates drew the line at how much affection he could legally show. They convicted both of them, fining the man £50 and giving his wife a conditional discharge.

Is nothing sacred? I always thought an Englishman's home was his castle.

"I've found someone for you to talk to, Mr. Henshaw."